Preyed on
or
Prayed for

Preyed on or Prayed for

Prayer Point Press

TO MY WIFE, KAY,
WHO ALWAYS MADE SURE I WAS PRAYED FOR.

CONTENTS

PREFACE

What a rare blessing it is indeed when God raises up a prophetic voice to speak with surgical precision to a specific need in the body. The need—the prayer of the saints for a beleaguered modern clergy facing unprecedented satanic assault.

The voice is Dr. Terry Teykl. Dr. Teykl has grasped the unique character of this attack as few have and with empathetic poignancy calls the house to order. It is high time we heed this appeal for effectual prayer protection for contemporary ministers. The scandal-ridden, demoralized, discouraged ranks of western clergymen are sad testimony of prayerless churches who virtually invite demonic attack on their pastors.

This is not merely some dismal, diagnostic report, however, but an insightful blueprint for action. This book places within reach of the concerned a plan of action to meet headlong, in the power of the Spirit, a clear and present danger.

Mark Rutland, President

Southeastern College, Lakeland, Florida

Air is no more necessary to the lungs
than prayer is to the preacher.
It is absolutely necessary for the preacher to pray.
It is an absolute necessity
that the preacher be prayed for.
These two propositions are wedded into a union
which ought never to know any divorce:
The preacher must pray,
the preacher must be prayed for.
It will take all the praying he can do,
and all the praying he can get done,
to meet the fearful responsibilities
and gain the largest, truest success
in his great work."

E. M. Bounds
The Complete Works of E. M. Bounds on Prayer

Introduction

The first piece of printed material I created to help people pray for their pastors was a half page prayer guide based on Ephesians 6. The idea came to me sitting in the back of a Sunday school room in Abilene, Texas. I was preaching a revival there, and the pastor and his wife were still grieving over the recent loss of their son. The church was suffering, and he was losing ground. I had been studying the book of Ephesians for several weeks, and as I pondered their situation, the prayer guide just exploded in me. I scribbled it on the back of my sermon notes.

About a year later, I expanded the simple guide into a working manual titled "Hedging in the Pastor." It was typed on a typewriter and reproduced on the church copy machine, much to the chagrin of whoever kept track of paper use in those days. It had a pea green cardstock cover with a hand drawn picture of something I probably dreamed up, like a shield with a bunch of darts sticking out of it or a stick figure surrounded by a bunch of well-trimmed bushes. I don't even remember. We found a copy of it not too long ago in the process of moving our warehouse and had a good laugh—the same way you laugh at pictures of yourself taken ten years ago in a family photo album.

The first version of this work to be titled *Preyed On or Prayed For* was born in 1993. It was a short, practical workbook based on the original manual that told readers how and why they should build a prayer hedge around their pastor. Another year and a half later, it was expanded again into the book by the same title, and the two sold as companions for a while until the workbook was taken out of print in 1997.

To be revising this work again seems almost silly on some counts. But the truth is, this message is as alive in me today as it was the first time I preached it—probably more. It's like watching one of your children grow up, develop and mature. Since its conception, it has been a part of my ministry, sometimes in the forefront, other times taking a back seat to some new vision or idea, but always present. I think I would call it a lifelong sermon, one that God specifically called me into the ministry to preach again and again. And I do. I've probably delivered more exhortations on Exodus 17 (the story of Moses, Aaron and Hur) than any other single Bible text. It just never gets old.

When I wrote the original version of the book *Preyed On or Prayed For*, I was still serving at Aldersgate United Methodist Church, a church I started in College Station, Texas and pastored for 16 years. Since that time, God has called me into a full time teaching ministry aimed at raising up prayer in local churches across the country. I have known first-hand the perils of pastoring, and I have ministered to hundreds of other pastors who shared their pain with someone they thought they could trust—a visitor from out of town.

When I am teaching in a church and have an audience made up of laypeople sprinkled with pastors, one of my favorite things to do is bring the pastors and their spouses up to the altar to be prayed for and blessed. Without fail, this exchange between sheep and shepherds proves to be one of the most meaningful moments of the day, and it seldom occurs without tears from both sides. It is always amazing to me the healing that takes place as I lead the people in prayers of honor and blessing for their leaders, and as they lay hands on one another in corporate repentance for past abuses and hurts. Seeing pastors be ministered to by their people is holy and precious, and the presence of the Holy Spirit often lingers in the room long after the time of prayer is over. God smiles when his appointed representatives are cared for.

A WOODPECKER'S PRIDE

I heard a story about a woodpecker that was perched on the side of a telephone pole furiously pecking away at the wood. When suddenly, unknown to him, a bolt of lightning struck the pole just at the instant that he pecked his most powerful peck. The pole split right down the middle. Bewildered, the woodpecker surveyed the damage and thought, "I didn't know I had it in me!"

Since the birth of *Preyed On or Prayed For*, much has happened in the area of prayer for pastors and leaders. Awareness of the need is much higher today than it was even five years ago. While I might like to think this book has been a contributing factor to the growing number of prayed for pastors, the truth is that it has truly been a sovereign move of God within the body of Christ. The Spirit has awakened many believers to the importance of covering our spiritual leaders in prayer, and churches and ministries are taking notice. Major organizations such as Promise Keepers and Focus on the Family have made pastoral prayer an emphasis, and thousands of pastors all over the county are joining together to pray for each other in support groups and fellowships.

But while more shepherds today are being prayed for by their flocks, many still are not. An overwhelming number, in fact, are still struggling along feeling discouraged and lonely, isolated from the people they are trying to minister to. Many are under fire, wounded, and worn out from years of repeated abuse or neglect. Every week, across the denominations, pastors are forced out of their pulpits because they dared to confront sin, resist financial controllers, or make a strong moral stand. I receive several calls a month from pastors who are facing personal tragedies or belief crises and they have no place to turn. There is much work still to be done.

As you read this revised edition, whether it is new information or old hat to you, I hope that you will renew your commitment to pray for your pastor and the other pastors of your city. I pray that you will engage others to do the same, and that somewhere in these pages, the idea will reach out and grab you and compel you to act. Ask the Holy Spirit to speak to you as you read the chapters, reflect on the questions, and then begin praying the prayers contained in this book.

Your prayers make a difference. Collectively, as the body of Christ, I believe covering our shepherds with intercession is one of the most fundamental, yet powerful things we can do in our efforts to affect our communities with the gospel and restore the church to health. Won't you join me in seeing that your pastor becomes one who is prayed for, and not preyed on?

CHAPTER ONE

PASTORS:
The Inside Story

We pastors are all unique. The range of our personalities, philosophies and theologies is as diverse as in the rest of the human race. Like you, we have a tendency to highlight our strengths and be guarded in areas where we feel weak. We would rather be accepted than rejected, and we don't like feeling vulnerable or embarrassed. When we stand in front of our congregations on Sunday mornings, chances are we're doing our best to have it "all together."

However, because most of us are reluctant to lower our defenses, especially in the pulpit, a lot of people think we don't live in the "real world."

Believe me, I feel confident speaking for pastors everywhere, living problem-free is not one of the perks of this job. When we signed on, we were given no guarantees that life would be easier just because we were

1. WRITE DOWN TWO OR THREE THINGS THAT YOUR PASTOR LIKES TO DO THAT HAVE NOTHING TO DO WITH MINISTRY.

2. IF YOU DON'T ALREADY KNOW, FIND OUT WHEN AND HOW YOUR PASTOR WAS CALLED INTO THE MINISTRY. RECORD A BRIEF SUMMARY OF WHAT YOU LEARN.

going to be in ministry. In fact, somewhere in the fine print, I think there must have been several health and sanity warnings, but most of us paid no attention to these.

Not only are we susceptible to all the same trials and difficulties that "normal" people face, but we get to be watched and evaluated as we deal with them. Remember the movies of the 1950s and 1960s that showed a priest who got so mad he said something "secular" or took a punch at the villain? You could almost hear the audience cheer! We are expected to be real and approachable, yet at the same time, surreal and above reproach. Life for pastors is a balancing act.

As a layperson, your mental image of your pastor is probably one of preaching, baptizing, conducting weddings, counseling couples and performing other duties required to fulfill his vows. It's likely you don't think much about your pastor balancing his personal checking account, disciplining the kids, arguing with his spouse, hunting like crazy for a lost shoe, or taking a day off to pursue a favorite hobby.

As I travel and speak, I have heard the heart cries of hundreds of pastors as they have shared with me their pains, aspirations, shortcomings and accomplishments. And while I can't give you the inside scoop on your pastor, hopefully I can make you aware that he has a personality that is played out behind the closed doors of the parsonage. I can also share with you several key things that all of the pastors I have come to know on a personal basis have in common.

> *[Your pastor] has a personality that is played out behind the closed doors of the parsonage.*

EIGHT THINGS ALL PASTORS HAVE IN COMMON

1. A Call to Ministry

John Wesley felt his heart "strangely warmed," and knew immediately that God had chosen him. A young man from Georgia related to me how, while walking in the woods, whistling the tune to "What a Friend We Have in Jesus," he felt "called." A college student from Seattle told about being visited by the Holy Spirit in a dream:

"I was awakened and sat up in bed," she said. "The entire room was filled with a presence I had never before known. I knew in my heart that God was calling me to lead others to the light." Personally, I was called into ministry while praying on top of my dog's house in our back yard! Ask any group of pastors how they were called to ministry, and they will tell you about some of the most memorable, inspiring experiences of their lives.

2. The Desire to Make a Difference

I have never met a pastor who did not, at least in the initial stages of her ministry, have a sincere desire to see lives changed as a result of her efforts. Some have a heart for seeing marriages restored, while others have a burden to feed and clothe the poor. Some feel specially called to comfort the sick; others have a vision for bringing the body of Christ to unity. Whatever your pastor's unique passion, be it global missions, inner-city outreach, discipleship training or family building, there is a good chance that it is driven by a fundamental yearning to see people come to know Jesus in a personal and life-altering way.

This is a very important point because of the insight it offers into why pastors burn out. While seeing lives changed by the gospel motivates most pastors, *not* seeing lives changed will eventually wear on them. Their work will become a laborious task instead of a joyful journey when months and years go by without visible fruit.

3. High Moments of Affirmation

Every pastor has "mountaintop" experiences that become the highlights of his ministry—an entire family receives Jesus and is baptized, a hardened sinner turns his life around as a result of the church's outreach, a marriage is restored through pastoral counseling. For small, rural church pastors and large, mega church pastors alike, ministry has its moments when the price paid pales in comparison to the eternal result. Marrying a young couple, dedicating a newborn baby, welcoming new members into the church family—these are the times when it's easy for a pastor to love what she does. The wind is blowing the right way. God is present. The pastor has a sensation of soaring on wings like eagles, running and not growing weary, walking and not fainting.

Few callings in life offer even close to the sheer joy and fulfillment of pastoring God's people. Although I no longer have my own church, I still have the privilege of preaching and ministering in local churches across the country. And every time I see someone saved, or feel the tears of a new convert on my own shoulder, I get a lump in my throat and goose bumps up and down my arms. When I can, I keep pictures of these precious people and events in my wallet or Bible as a reminder of why I do what I do. These are moments of unprecedented significance in my life, and they not only affirm my commitment to serve God, but they encourage me when things get tough.

4. *Low Moments of Frustration*

And things do get tough for those who minister. Maybe it's something simple—like the times a pastor has to choose between taking one of her children to a special event at school, and visiting a surgery patient in the hospital. Or, it can be more complicated, like dealing with a moral mistake of a staff member or an emotionally charged issue that is threatening to divide the church. Regardless, frustration is inevitable.

For example, a pastor from Kansas cut short his long-overdue family vacation and drove all night to get home in time to conduct the funeral of one of his dearest members.

3. WRITE DOWN THE NAMES OF YOUR PASTOR'S FAMILY MEMBERS AND A LITTLE ABOUT EACH ONE (AGE, WHAT THEY DO, ETC.).

4. BASED ON WHAT YOU KNOW, WHAT IS YOUR PASTOR'S PARTICULAR PASSION IN MINISTRY?

The family sat quietly until, during the eulogy, he announced with unbridled admiration that the deceased had left her entire estate to the church. Relatives seated in the family section were visibly shaken and many began to cry in a way that surpassed normal expressions of grief at the loss of a loved one. Their tears quickly turned to anger.

As the pall bearers were carrying the casket out of the church, the pastor heard the deceased woman's son tell his sister that they had been "done in" by the pastor. Later, as the son walked away from the grave-side ceremony, he turned to the pastor and, with tears streaming down his face and a stony chill in his voice, said, "I'll see you in court, preacher!"

The following week, the pastor received notification from another church in his city that six of his most loyal members had transferred their memberships to a sister denomination.

5. The Fear of Failure

In spite of the fact that most pastors would like to preach the word of God, unabated and uncensored, many consistently water down their messages for fear of alienating some of their members whose support they feel is vital to their mission. Convicted sheep can make a shepherd's life miserable! When your wife has friends in a community and your children are doing well in school, the last thing you want to do is rock the boat. Nothing is more dreaded than the Monday morning phone call, "Pastor, you know we all do our best to support you as much as we can, but you said something yesterday that has some of us a little concerned...." Oh, the "We love you, *but...*" message! Any pastor who has heard that conversation starter knows that it goes downhill from there. He might as well call U-haul. As one observer said, "It's not a good idea for a pastor to get too close to the fire. He might get burned!"

As much as pastors fear offending parishioners, there are other dreaded stigmas of failure—declining membership, transfer to a smaller church, rejection by other pastors in the community. It's amazing to me that even pastors who would be considered very successful on all counts, are often deeply, painfully insecure and desperately afraid of failing. According to one survey, 90 percent of today's clergy feel they were inadequately trained to cope with the high demands of ministry, while 50 percent feel unable to meet the current needs of their job (Ells). Their fear may be the very thing that drives them to put in long hours at the church, make great personal sacrifices at the expense of their family's well-being, and generally try to be everything to everybody all the time.

6. Clay Feet

Although it should be rather obvious, it bears stating: pastors are only human. Yes, they have a divine calling on their lives to fill a spiritual leadership role, and they are often referred to as "holy men and women of God," but they struggle with all of the same temptations, weaknesses and pitfalls that the rest of us do. At times they march in

5. LIST CHARACTERISTICS OF YOUR PASTOR THAT YOU CONSIDER TO BE STRENGTHS.

6. IN WHAT AREAS OR FROM WHAT SPECIFIC GROUPS DO YOU THINK YOUR PASTOR MIGHT FEEL NEGATIVE PRESSURE?

7. IS ANYONE CURRENTLY PRAY-
ING REGULARLY FOR YOUR SHEP-
HERD? WRITE DOWN THE DETAILS.

victory and at times they stumble along in hidden, personal defeat.

Your pastor may wrestle with a love of money, unholy thoughts, an explosive temper, pride, unforgiveness, or even a distrust of God. Throughout his years in ministry, he will no doubt suffer at least a tinge of "meltdown" in some area of his spiritual life. Consider some of the followers of Jesus who actually spent personal time with the Savior: Paul struggled with attitudes about women, Thomas with doubt, Peter with impetuousness. As a group they struggled often with fear and disbelief; at times they didn't even understand Jesus' mission, despite the fact that he lived and taught among them.

The tragic stories of faithful ministers who fall into depression, disillusionment or moral scandal do not happen overnight. A sincere pastor does not wake up one morning and say, "I think I'll throw away everything I believe in today" and then jump headlong into a crisis. He loses his footing one small decision at a time, shaken by some common temptation in an area where he is weak. That is why this book is so important for you to read and implement, even if your pastor does not appear to have any visible problems. Your prayers will make the difference when he is faced with that benign looking opportunity to compromise or stand firm.

7. Lack of Prayer Training

When I speak to a group of pastors, one of my favorite questions to ask is, "How many of you received at least one course on prayer in your ministry training?" Usually, no more than one or two hands go up. It is an unfortunate reality that most of our semi-naries have been and are still sorely lacking in the area of prayer curriculum and train-ing, which means we have a nation full of churches led by individuals who don't really understand the basics of prayer, nor how to train their people to do it. In general, our clergy in this country are uninformed about

> *At times they march in victory and at times they stumble along in hidden, personal defeat.*

such things as the relationship between prayer and evangelism, the global prayer movement, trends in city-wide prayer, the importance of prayer as a ministry in the local church, and the need for prayer for leaders.

Over the past several years, we have begun to see a shift that holds some promise in the realm of prayer education for pastors. Several minis-try training programs have popped up in local churches that are, as a rule, at least somewhat prayer-based, offering an alternative to the traditional seminary route. While such programs can't offer certified degrees, they are turning out graduates who are more equipped in the practical areas of ministry, including prayer, since their training ground is actually in the trenches of a thriving local church. The students are giving up courses in Greek, Hebrew, escatology, and church history in lieu of on-the-job expe-rience in staff management, budgeting, administration and spiritual de-velopment.

One such program is at New Life Church in Colorado Springs where the church basically raises its own ministers by bringing hand-picked candidates up through the ranks as small group leaders, interns and associates. For senior pastor Ted Haggard, it is the only way to go.

8. *The Need for Spiritual Support From Laypersons*

Whether they realize it or not, all pastors need support from laypeople, most especially in the form of consistent, intentional prayer. That is what this book is about.

It is about building a guard rail around the sharp turns of the ministry mountain rather than parking an ambulance at the bottom to catch those who fall. It is not about how much you like your pastor, or even whether you always agree with everything he says. Rather, it's about recognizing the spiritual nature of the office of pastor, and honoring God by praying diligently for the men and women he has chosen to represent him in that office. Not only are pastors' lives at stake, but so is the kingdom agenda to which they are committed.

WHY PASTORS DON'T ASK FOR PRAYER

As you begin to think about organizing prayer for your pastor, you need to be aware that you may not get her whole-hearted cooperation. Although it sounds strange, your pastor may be less than enthusiastic about your efforts, and may actually resist receiving prayer at first. If it is a new idea, it will take some adjusting to. Ironically, sometimes the pastor is the least prayed-for person in the local church. She may live in a nice house and receive good pay, yet be neglected in the prayers of the flock.

C. Peter Wagner has an excellent chapter in his book *Prayer Shield* on receiving intercession (104-116). As he encourages pastors to become more open in seeking prayer support, he discusses several reasons why they often won't. The following is a summary of these roadblocks to accepting prayer.

A. *Ignorance*

Often, pastors just don't think to ask for prayer on a regular basis. They may ask for prayer on special occasions, for specific preaching missions or at troubled times in their ministry, but it may not be something they think about needing on a regular basis. They will ask for financial support or for time commitments from their flocks before they will ask for daily or weekly prayer. It

> *[This book] is about building a guard rail around the sharp turns of the ministry mountain rather than parking an ambulance at the bottom....*

may not have been emphasized in seminary or it's not the traditional thing to do. It is amazing how much has been written on recovery and personal development for pastors, yet the idea of prayer as a preventative has been sorely neglected in the majority of this literature. Even in the years that have ensued since the original publication of this book, little has been written on the importance of prayer for leaders, despite the progress in awareness.

For example, George Barna's book, *Today's Pastors*, is an excellent resource for information about senior pastors across the country and where they stand as a profession in their own eyes as well as in the eyes of their congregations. He found some startling statistics about frustrations, fears and struggles that pastors face in ministry. He even offered some reasons for such conditions as well as some possible solutions. But nowhere in his analysis did prayer for pastors show up.

It seems that raising up prayer hedges for the shepherds of our nation is a solution that is just being discovered and taken seriously. It is an educational battle that this book was written to help fight. I have seen laypeople respond once they understand the need and hear their pastor say, "Pray for me—I need your covering to survive!"

B. Rugged Individualism

Many pastors are not prayed for because they like to think of themselves as being "rugged individualists." They feel they are supposed to have the answers. "Look to us," they say, "and we will pray and speak the message from God." Fallen leaders abound who tried to be completely self-sufficient and were not open to expose the needs for prayer. Jimmy Swaggart reflected on this when he said:

> I think this is the reason that I did not find the victory I sought because I did not seek the help of my brothers and my sisters in the Lord.... If I had sought the help of those that love me, with their added strength, I look back now and know that the victory would have been mine (Wagner, *Shield* 109).

...until we offer pastors a safe, consistent place to communicate their personal and ministerial needs, they can not receive the prayer they so desperately need.

For pastors, it is easy to fall into the mentality that says, "I don't need anyone's help. I just need God." It can be difficult to step beyond the chancel rail with humility and say, "I'm counting on your prayers because I can't do this under my own strength." But it is imperative for every pastor to be able to share his heart with a core of people he trusts. There are some who can pray over general requests and others who can be trusted with more intimate concerns. But the bottom line is, until we offer pastors a safe, consistent place to communicate their personal and ministerial needs, they can not receive the prayer they so desperately need. Barna's assessment is painfully true when he states:

In the typical church, it is impossible for the pastor to
be truly transparent about the struggles he endures with
people within the church, within his family or within
the ministry overall. Consequently, most pastors tell us
they feel lonely in ministry. While they have many friends
and acquaintances with whom they can share a good
laugh and a pleasant evening, they have few people with
whom they can share their hearts (145).

When I pastored, I had several levels of intercessors. A small group
of men prayed with me intimately. Another 20 men prayed for me during
Sunday's ministry. I met with them on Sunday mornings and shared my
text and my goals so they could pray effectively. In our prayer room, there
was a recorder on which I shared my needs and concerns on a weekly
basis, and I had an Aaron and Hur Society that prayed for me on an ongoing basis. On special occasions, my close friends in the ministry prayed
for me. But in every case, it was up to me to lay aside my pride and
introverted tendencies and communicate.

C. Fear

For many pastors, fear is a huge stumbling block to receiving prayer.
They are afraid that what they say might be used against them, and for
good reason. Many pastors can remember at least one time when they
confided in a parishioner or another church leader with disastrous results
(Ells). Experience tells them that if they let people see their weaknesses
and needs—their humanness—they will lose the confidence of their flocks.
Pastors reason, "What if my prayer requests are misunderstood or taken
the wrong way? What if word gets out that I am struggling in this area?
Will I still be respected as a spiritual leader?" Fear to ask for help when
needed has caused too many pastors to end up living lives of regret.

Fear is the number one dart the enemy shoots at pastors. It is a
versatile weapon, able to injure and paralyze in many ways.

8. WOULD YOUR ATTITUDE TO-
WARD YOUR PASTOR CHANGE IF YOU
LEARNED THAT HE WAS FACING A
SERIOUS PERSONAL CRISIS, SUCH AS
MARITAL PROBLEMS, A CHILD ON
DRUGS, OR A GAMBLING HABIT?

9. HOW DO YOU THINK GOD
WANTS THE CHURCH TO RESPOND
TO A SHEPHERD WITH THESE (OR
SIMILAR) DIFFICULTIES? FIND SCRIP-
TURES TO SUPPORT YOUR OPINION.

Some pastors fear failure, not knowing what they would do outside of pastoring. Others are terrified of the opinions of peers or denominational leaders. Some pastors are afraid to take stands on social issues such as drinking or abortion.

Proverbs 29:25 is right: "Fear of man will prove to be a snare." Prolonged fear in a pastor will undermine confidence and squelch boldness in the Holy Spirit. It will make him sick, depressed and cynical. The more fearful he is, the more vulnerable and ineffective he will be as a spiritual leader.

Consider the role that fear played in the following tragedy:

Because Betty was raised in upstate New York, she had a difficult time fitting in when her husband, John, was assigned to pastor a church in the south. She never felt accepted, and was constantly battling depression and loneliness.

Her condition got so bad that just before their first Christmas there, John had to hospitalize her for an overdose of sleeping pills. After returning home, she sensed that everyone in the church knew what had happened. She even overheard one of the members telling his son that she was "nuts."

John wanted desperately to help his wife—he knew the situation was getting serious. But he also yearned for the approval of his new congregation. The tension at the church because of his wife's difficulties was already making things hard on them, and his tendency was to try to play it down. He was too afraid of being misunderstood or criticized to even ask for prayer. He reasoned that revealing the severity of her condition would only make things worse by drawing attention to the matter.

Then one morning, as John prepared to leave town for a pastors' conference, Betty confided in him, "Honey, the people in the hospital were so nice to me. Why are the people in our church so cruel?"

John tried to reassure her, "I'm sure they don't mean it. Things will be better after the holidays. Once they get to know you, everything will be just fine." But even he didn't believe what he was saying.

Just hours later, as John backed out of the driveway, Betty decided to write him a letter explaining how she had decided to stop her pain.

"Urgent—Call your church." That's all that was written on the note John received the following morning as he ate breakfast with fellow pastors. When he returned the call, he learned that his wife had ended her life. Late the previous evening, Betty had entered the sanctuary and taken what the letter found by her body described as her "last communion," a massive dose of sleeping pills.

The tragic thing about this situation is that despite the fact that many people in the church would have been willing to support their pastor and his wife through their crisis, he was unable to ask for or accept help because he feared exposure and embarrassment. Think of the suffering and loss that might have been avoided, or at least lessened, if John had been able to share his burden with a group of dedicated intercessors and receive prayer. Imagine how a strong and loving network of prayer support might have changed Betty's outlook.

As you read this book, begin praying for your shepherd right away. Don't wait for a crisis or to have everything perfectly organized. Do everything you can to begin building your pastor's trust so that you are never faced with the question, "What if...?"

D. Spiritual Arrogance

Pride can be so subtle in a pastor, especially the longer they serve and the more "experienced" they are. I can testify from first-hand knowledge that pastors are tempted every day to put their trust in their seminary degrees, their gifts and talents, their past successes or their noteworthy reputations. No pastor is immune to spiritual arrogance because it is one of Satan's oldest and most effective tools for knocking godly leaders off course. He even tried to use it against Jesus.

Remember when Jesus was in the desert for forty days? After the devil had unsuccessfully tried to tempt Jesus with food and wealth, his last resort was to appeal to Jesus' sense of pride. "Go on," he said, "jump off the temple. After all, if you are the 'son of God,' he will command the angels to save you and the people will be so impressed! You'll be more famous than ever!" He was tempting Jesus to rely on his resources and show off his very cool, divine flying skills. Of course, Jesus knew better.

Spiritual arrogance in senior pastors can sometimes take the form of an excessive need for control. Because they often have administrative and leadership qualities anyway, they can struggle with wanting to control everything that goes on in their churches.

Asking people to pray for you requires vulnerability and openness. It is this very dynamic that can protect pastors from arrogance, pride and self-sufficiency. If you think your pastor may be suffering under the weight of spiritual arrogance, take your concern to God. Let him do the work necessary to bring your shepherd back to a place of true humility and dependence.

E. Undue Humility

Finally, Wagner says that undue humility can prevent pastors from being prayed for. He states:

> The logic goes something like this: "I am no better than anyone else in the body of Christ. We are all sinners saved by grace. God loves all of his children equally. He does not love me any more than the others. Why, then, should I expect to receive this powerful intercession when so many of my church members do not have the same privilege? Instead of building a special team of prayer partners for myself, might it not be bet-

10. ASK GOD TO SHOW YOU WHY YOUR OWN PASTOR MAY FIND IT DIFFICULT TO ASK FOR PRAYER. BEGIN PRAYING FOR GOD TO DO WHATEVER WORK IS NECESSARY IN YOUR SHEPHERD'S HEART.

ter to just encourage all church members to pray for
each other? (*Shield* 115)

Humility is a very Christlike quality and a sign of spiritual maturity.
It becomes something else, however, when it prevents a person from seeking help or developing healthy relationships. When a person becomes so
"humble" that she can not accept a compliment or see any value in herself and her God-given abilities, then she is suffering from "false humility," which is not from God. A truly humble person is able to acknowledge
both strengths and weaknesses, secure in the understanding of her worth
in Christ and keenly aware of her dependence on him.

It is true that pastors are ordinary people, but they have an extraor-
dinary call to preach and lead the church—the bride of Christ. It is a
spiritual task that requires power and wisdom that only the Holy Spirit
can give. For this reason, they need a special prayer covering. To the
same degree that we are willing to intercede in their behalf, God will ex-
tend his hand of provision and protection to them and around them.

But our pastors will not be the only beneficiaries of our prayers.
When we pray for them, we get to go with them when they go to prisons or
hospitals. We become a part of their day-to-day ministry and preaching.
When this happens, we will truly become joint heirs in the service of
Jesus Christ. As we pray for shepherds, we reap the same blessings that
they do when souls are saved and lives are changed. Their victory becomes our victory because prayer paved the way for the harvest.

START NOW

George Barna is right in asking:

Is it time to evaluate how satisfactorily the current church
ministry system cares for pastors? Do we need to deter-
mine how well we are looking after the financial, emo-

tional, and spiritual welfare of our spiritual leaders...?"
(*Pastors* 40)

The answers to these questions are "Yes!" If you are not already doing it, it is time to begin evaluating how well your pastoral family is being "looked after." Do not expect them to ask for help, and more importantly, don't wait until there is a crisis.

Take a few minutes before reading further to ask God to give you his mind and heart for pastors:

> *Dear Lord, put your heart in me for all the men and women who have committed their lives to serving you. Let me see them through your eyes, the eyes of a proud and compassionate Father. Reveal to me the beauty you see in their diversity—light, dark, young, old, educated, innocent, gifted and humble. As I read this book, talk to me, Spirit to spirit, so that I will understand how important this is to you. Thank you for my pastor. Forgive me for any wrong thoughts or attitudes I might have had in the past toward him or her. Teach me how to pray effectively for my shepherd. In Jesus' name, Amen.*

CHAPTER TWO

SHEEP CAN _____
Bite!

Had the pastor of a Baptist church in Houston not dropped by the church late one evening to pick something up from his office, he might never have known the danger he was in. As he walked past the sanctuary doors, he heard a noise, and peeked inside to see what was going on at such an odd hour. What he saw was six of his newest members dressed in black, sitting in a half circle facing the pulpit area. Curiously, he watched for a moment. "That is no prayer meeting!" he thought to himself.

When he questioned the six, they readily admitted that they were all members of a satanic cult, and they had been assigned to undermine his ministry and devastate his church. That night, as they had many nights since they "joined" the church, they were holding a satanic ritual, calling upon the forces of evil to prevail. Their primary target...the pastor.

Satan is the antithesis of everything Jesus Christ stands for, and he loves to hate pastors. He is a liar and a master of disguise. His most cunning work in churches is done not through demons in the organ, but rather through people whose hearts are not turned toward the things of God. He uses weapons of distrust, skepticism, disunity, seduction, coercion, depression, self-doubt and disaster.

Most New Testament-inspired paintings of sheep are rather idyllic. You have a shepherd overlooking some white, fluffy, lovable lambs. Remember the scene of a shepherd carrying a little lamb on his shoulders while the other sheep gaze up at him with an "isn't that nice" look in their eyes? However, Dr. Mark Rutland reminds us that sheep can bite. In fact, they can knock a pastor down, stomp on him, and drag him into the bushes for dead. Any pastor who has tried to change the service times, rearrange the order of worship, or move the piano to make room for a guitar knows this to be true! You can go to any denominational preachers' meeting and see first hand the scars and teeth marks left by irate sheep.

> *...sheep can bite. In fact, they can knock a pastor down, stomp on him, and drag him into the bushes for dead.*

THE PERILS OF PASTORING

One of the enemy's most effective tools for sucking the life out of pastors and their churches is pettiness, or "majoring in minors." Pettiness is a church staff arguing over who ordered candles without permission, or a disgruntled parent complaining because someone else's child was chosen to sing the choir solo. It can be the fruit of personal pride, insecurity or fear, and is usually tied to issues of control. Consider, for example, my friend Carlos.

A compassionate, middle-aged preacher, Carlos has always had a special burden for ministering to people who have disabilities. Wherever he has pastored, he has always encouraged parents of children with special needs to bring them into the worship service.

One morning as Carlos was preaching, a 12-year-old boy who was mentally challenged jumped up from his pew and ran up to the pulpit. He didn't make a lot of noise or even interrupt the sermon, but for the remainder of the service, he stood alongside the pastor with a big grin on his face.

> *One of the enemy's most effective tools for sucking the life out of pastors and their churches is pettiness, or "majoring in minors."*

Some of the members were visibly upset. As one man was leaving the sanctuary, he expressed his displeasure to Carlos. "That boy disrupted the entire service. We should not tolerate such behavior in the house of God!" Others were quick to agree.

Although Carlos was confident in God's calling on his life, he could not, despite sincere attempts, enlighten his congregation. He was forced to deal with what he soon learned was a well-organized telephone campaign to keep him under control.

Another pastor in Virginia faced a similar struggle when he put a prayer room in his church. Within weeks, he discovered that one of the members adamantly opposed it. On Palm Sunday, this woman took the microphone without permission and said, "I oppose this prayer room idea for the following reasons: If we use the proposed room we'll have nowhere to put the hand bells; my sister will have nowhere to hang her organ robe; someone might trip getting into the prayer room; and, someone might get raped in there!"

The congregation began to laugh until they realized she was serious. She and her family left the church, but not before saying and doing all they could to make the pastor "pay" for his decision.

1. DO YOU AGREE WITH THE IDEA THAT PETTINESS IS A COMMON PROBLEM FOR PASTORS AND CHURCHES?

2. WHY IS PETTINESS RELATED TO CONTROL ISSUES IN A CHURCH OR ANY ORGANIZATIONAL STRUCTURE?

In Richmond, Indiana, a pastor got excited during her sermon one morning and jumped up and down and came out from behind the pulpit. The next week she was called on the carpet. Five "controllers" told her, "We do not have shows of enthusiasm like that in our church, and our preachers stay behind the pulpit."

Another friend, after lifting the offering plates up over the altar one Sunday, was told he was being too dramatic. A pastor in Phoenix was given a list of people not to visit, lest they come to church. A pastor in east Texas was accused of having a hobby that cost too much. I have sat in board meetings with a sick feeling in my stomach watching power struggles over what kind of disposable cups to use for fellowship dinners! Does any of this make sense?

The enemy majors in pettiness to keep pastors drained and distracted from the real issue of taking cities for God. The question "Who's in charge here?" is a spiritual one. The problem is really not the color of the carpet or which hymnal to use, the problem is a lack of spiritual understanding.

All of these pastors felt hurt and betrayed by the flocks they were trying to serve. Their ministries were damaged by petty insecurities and self-serving interests. What they needed were prayer hedges made up of the spiritually mature members who supported their visions. Such prayer covering might not have warded off the attacks, but it certainly would have altered the long-range effects.

Don't wait for a crisis to muster your troops to pray. If you are caught scrambling to organize prayer for your pastor in the heat of battle, you will lose a lot of ground before you even get started—and the stakes are too high. Pastoring is, and always has been, perilous.

LESSONS FROM THE NEW TESTAMENT

The New Testament is certainly clear about the perils of pastoring. Yet it is amazing how we neglect to study these teachings. Instead we focus on things we find easier to understand, such as the qualifications for church leadership and the requirements of personal holiness.

The book of Acts abounds with examples of church leadership being both attacked and blessed under the pressure of a growing ministry. Paul wrote, "I only know that in every city the Holy Spirit warns me that prison and hardships are facing me" (Acts 20:23). In 2 Corinthians 6:4-10, he added:

> Rather, as servants of God we commend ourselves in every way: in great endurance; ...in beatings, imprisonments and riots; in hard work, sleepless nights and hunger; in purity, understanding, patience and kindness; in the Holy Spirit and in sincere love; in truthful speech and in the power of God; with weapons of righteousness in the right hand and in the left; through glory and dishonor, bad report and good report; genuine, yet regarded as impostors; ...dying, yet we live on; beaten,

and yet not killed; sorrowful, yet always rejoicing; poor, yet making many rich; having nothing and yet possessing everything.

In these passages, Paul paralleled the blessings with the hardships, the qualifications with the pressures of shepherding, the good with the bad. It is no easy road to be a pastor at any time in any place. Any view of leadership that neglects the consequences of being a pastor is a truncated model. If there were no perils, pressures or persecutions, prayer would not be needed. The Bible teaches—and even guarantees—pressures and problems with the blessings of pastoring. Therefore, a protective prayer hedge for the pastor is essential.

> *The Bible teaches—and even guarantees—pressures and problems with the blessings of pastoring.*

A CLASH OF KINGDOMS

" Please cancel the prayer seminar." That's the request of a letter I received concerning a scheduled prayer seminar in south Alabama that I wanted very much to conduct. "I can't handle it," the pastor wrote.

He told me he had experienced a personal revival at a renewal conference earlier that year which had given him new vision for his church's future. He had been preaching on the person and work of the Holy Spirit, calling his people to embrace a fresh expressions of evangelism and worship. Then, he dropped the bombshell.

"What I managed to do was stir up both that which is wonderful and that which is both ugly and painful. It is not the time for a prayer conference. I have much opposition to it. My future here is uncertain and I must be sensitive to God's backing one day at a time. I covet your prayers and trust that you understand my need to cancel."

Sure, I can read between the lines. It was the proverbial "clash of kingdoms" that every pastor learns to work around just to stay on the job! What else could he have done?

The New Testament mandate to pray for pastors is necessary for a very good reason: the gospel is confrontational. It was then, and it is now. The gospel of Jesus continually calls people to new life, new convictions, new power, a new fruitfulness, a new set of values, a new way of looking at people and a new freedom. Jesus calls us to leave the old and cling to the new. He was the one who gave us a new commandment and a new covenant. He offers a new life and a new way. In Revelation 21:5, Jesus said, "I am making everything new." The gospel is always the new movement of God, and pastors are the messengers.

The gospel confronts sin and beckons repentance and holiness, and it is planted in us to bear new fruit. Paul wrote to the Colossians, "All over the world this gospel is producing fruit and growing, just as it has been doing among you since the day you heard it and understood God's grace in all its truth" (1:6).

> *"There is nothing same, lame or tame about the gospel."*

John Ogilvie, now chaplain for the United States Senate, used to say, "There is nothing same, lame or tame about the gospel."

Because it is confrontational, the gospel often results in a clash of kingdoms. Dudley Hall says in his book *Out of the Comfort Zone* that the people of the old move of God can fight or resist the people of the new move of God.

History bears witness to this principle again and again. The new reign and rule of Jesus Christ clashed with the old reign of sin and religion. The gospel of light clashes with the kingdom of darkness. Quite

3. WHAT DOES THE PHRASE "CLASH OF KINGDOMS" MEAN TO YOU?

4. HAVE YOU EVER SEEN THE OLD ORDER RESIST THE NEW MOVE OF GOD IN A CHURCH? WHAT WAS THE OUTCOME?

often the pastor gets caught in the crossfire and is crushed in between the conflicting ideologies.

BLESSED AND BATTERED: THE STORY OF ACTS

An overview of the New Testament reveals that pastors are blessed and battered—hands are laid on to ordain, and they are laid on to kill. Paul wrote in his first letter to the Corinthians, "...but I will stay on at Ephesus until Pentecost, because a great door for effective work has opened to me, and there are many who oppose me" (16:8-9). Therefore, he admonished them, "Be on your guard, stand firm in the faith; be men of courage; be strong" (16:13).

The book of Acts is especially useful for understanding some of the perils of pastoring, and the turmoil that can be stirred up when people start responding to the gospel.

Changed Lives and Death Threats

A changed life is an indictment of an unchanged life, and an indictment generally creates guilt or anger. Unfortunately, it is often the pastor that becomes the target for retaliation.

In Acts 16, Paul and Silas encountered a young slave girl. The Bible tells us that she "had a spirit by which she predicted the future," and that "she earned a great deal of money for her owners by fortune-telling" (verse 16). Paul prayed for her, she was immediately delivered and saved, and her life was completely changed. When her owners realized that their fortune-telling fortunes had just gone down the drain, they got angry. They seized Paul and Silas and dragged them into the market place, where they were stripped, beaten severely and cast into prison.

There are at least six other instances in Acts where pastors were put in prison for preaching. Such are the results of proclaiming a life-changing Savior.

It is estimated that in the first five chapters of Acts, more than 20,000 people came to the Lord. Can you imagine a pastor trying to get these names written on the official roll? Just think about ordering children's literature for all these new families. In almost every chapter, lives were changed by Jesus Christ. People fell under conviction, repented and were baptized. The pastors were blessed and the church expanded. However, for every person who did repent, there were many who fought this new truth about Jesus.

In Acts 9, Paul was radically transformed on the road to Damascus. He received a new life in Christ, and he immediately began to testify for Jesus. He grew more and more powerful in bearing witness. Then we read in verse 23, "After many days had gone by, the Jews conspired to kill him...." This new pastor was in deep trouble! The old order did not buy his new message and new life, and their solution was to wipe him out. So Paul became a "basket case," and escaped through a hole in the wall (verse 25). His new life had not reflected favorably upon the lives of those who had rejected the gospel.

The Tensions of New Convictions

The Acts of the Apostles also reveal the tensions caused by the new and bold convictions of Jesus Christ. Jesus calls us to believe in a new way, and sometimes even cherished doctrines must be confronted and called to change.

For example, in Christ, we believe new things about ourselves, God, and others. In Acts 4:2-4, many people heard and believed the message Peter and John preached and "the number of men grew to about five thousand." As a result, the Jews were "greatly disturbed," and they "seized Peter and John," threatening them to cease teaching this new doctrine of salvation by grace.

> *...sometimes even cherished doctrines must be confronted and called to change.*

The same was true in Acts 6 and 7, when Pastor Stephen preached a new conviction which called for receiving Jesus Christ as the Messiah. They seized him, and brought him before the Sanhedrin. When they heard this pastor's convictions, "they were furious and gnashed their teeth at him," and they all "rushed at him, dragged him out of the city and began to stone him" (Acts 7:54, 57-58).

In Acts 13, we see another example of the clash between the old and new, thanks to Pastor Paul and Pastor Barnabas. They preached a new doctrine that the Gentiles could be saved, and many believed. We read, "When the Gentiles heard this, they were glad and honored the word of the Lord; and all who were appointed for eternal life believed. The word of the Lord spread through the whole region" (Acts 13:48-49). Some people, however, refused to change their convictions: "But the Jews incited the God-fearing women of high standing and the leading men of the city. They stirred up persecution against Paul and Barnabas," and had them moved to another church! (verse 50)

Paul and Barnabas, like Peter, John and Stephen, got into trouble because of what they believed. When the Prince of all principles beckons us to a new conviction, the end result can be conflict for those who teach and follow Jesus Christ.

Revival and Riots

A third source of opposition to pastors that we see in the book of Acts is the new power released in believers through the Holy Spirit. As the pastors in Acts proclaimed the powerful name of Jesus, signs and wonders followed their preaching. People were healed and delivered. With this new power, they preached the word and many were saved. But not everyone was excited about the miracles. In essence, some of the early pastors got in trouble for being "too spiritual." The revivals they ignited usually incited riots of equal proportion.

Acts 14:3 tells us that Paul and Barnabas spoke "boldly for the Lord, who confirmed the message of his grace by enabling them to do miraculous signs and wonders." The end result was, "the Jews who refused to believe stirred up the Gentiles and poisoned their minds against the brothers" [pastors]. Many in the city conspired to mistreat Paul and Barnabas and stone them, forcing them to flee. (Acts 14:2, 5-6).

The same thing happened in Lystra. A man was healed and "some Jews came from Antioch and Iconium and won the crowd over. They stoned Paul and dragged him outside the city, thinking he was dead" (Acts 14:19).

Your pastor can get into trouble for praying for people in Jesus' name, especially when people are healed! A dead church is indicted by an alive church. The supernatural can upset a church whose norm is the natural. It is appropriate that the King James Version of the Bible calls the Holy Spirit the "Holy Ghost," for he tends to haunt a church that is trying

5. WHY WERE THE DISCIPLES TOLD TO STOP PREACHING IN THE NAME OF JESUS?

6. HOW DOES A PASTOR OPERATE IN THE "SAFE ZONE"? WHAT WOULD HAVE HAPPENED (OR NOT HAPPENED) IF PAUL AND THE OTHERS HAD OPERATED THERE?

to do things in its own strength!

Pastors who operate in the "safe zone" rarely get in trouble. It is the name of Jesus that causes a stir one way or the other. That is why in Acts 4:18 the rulers, elders and teachers called the pastors in and "commanded them not to speak or teach at all in the name of Jesus."

Jealous Jews

Jesus said in John 15:8, "This is to my Father's glory, that you bear much fruit, showing yourselves to be my disciples." This fruit provided another source of conflict for pastors in Acts, because the blessings caused by the gospel made the Jews jealous.

In Acts 5:16 we read, "Crowds gathered also from the towns around Jerusalem, bringing their sick and those tormented by evil spirits, and all of them were healed." As a result, "the high priest and all his associates...were filled with jealousy. They arrested the apostles (pastors) and put them in the public jail" (Acts 5:17-18). Later in Acts 13:44-45 we read, "On the next Sabbath almost the whole city gathered to hear the word of the Lord. When the Jews saw the crowds, they were filled with jealousy and talked abusively against what Paul was saying." Furthermore, when they saw the blessings that resulted from the gospel, they were indignant because the fruit of the gospel indicted their own lack of results.

These pastors got into trouble as the church grew and became a dynamic influence in the community. But that is not the end of the story. Paul moved to Thessalonica, where some of the Jews were persuaded to join Paul and Silas, "as did a large number of God-fearing Greeks and not a few prominent women" (Acts 17:4).

Again, the gospel produced results, and as before, "the Jews were jealous; so they rounded up some bad characters from the marketplace, formed a mob and started a riot in the city" (Acts 17:5). So Paul moved again, eventually going to Corinth, where Crispus, the synagogue ruler, believed along with many Corinthians (Acts 18:8). The consequences were the same. The Jews made yet another united attack on Paul (Acts 19:12) as a result of the blessings that were poured out when he preached Jesus Christ.

> *The gospel is confrontational. Where Jesus is preached, things happen—revival, riots, blessings and jealousy.*

The gospel is confrontational. Where Jesus is preached, things happen—revival, riots, blessings and jealousy. Jesus said, "This is to my Father's glory, that you bear much fruit...." The New Testament pastors learned that a growing, dynamic church that is blessed with much fruit will cause opposition and jealousy to arise. Often the attack will be aimed at the leader—the pastor.

Let's Accuse a Pastor!

Finally, the pastors in the New Testament came under attack from a spirit of accusation.

The gospel they preached called men and women to a new and bold affirmation. In Christ, people are commended before God based on the righteousness of Jesus and affirmed as being set free from the law. In Christ, people are declared forgiven, redeemed and healed. They are under grace: "...if anyone is in Christ, he is a new creation; the old has gone, the new has come!" (2 Corinthians 5:17)

For the law-lovers, this was not good news. They radically opposed this new teaching of grace because it was hurting their business and undermining their influence. And since they could find no legitimate faults with the disciples or their message, they did the next best thing—they made some up.

The pastors in Acts were accused often and unjustly. In Acts 6, Stephen was accused by the religious teachers of "speaking against" their holy place, the synagogue, and against the law. But because these angry teachers "could not stand up against his wisdom or the Spirit by which he spoke," they had to secretly persuade some other men to make the accusation by using false witness.

In Acts 16, Paul and Silas were accused of starting a riot in the city by advocating customs unlawful for the Romans to practice. Ironically, though, the very ones who brought the accusation were those who actually started the riot!

Later in Acts 19, Paul was accused of undermining the temple of the goddess Artemis. A silversmith, who made a good income by building shrines for the temple, convinced his men that Paul was not only a threat to their financial success, but that he also was discrediting the goddess. The men became furious. Then in chapter 21, Pastor Paul, like Stephen, was accused of defiling the holy place and he was arrested.

Acts 25:7 reveals the force and energy of the accusations against Paul: "When Paul appeared, the Jews who had come down from Jerusalem stood around him, bringing many serious charges against him, which they could not prove." Everywhere Paul went, mud started flying.

Because the world thrives on rumors and half-truths, accusation is one of the most lethal weapons that can be used against a pastor. The sad reality is, even the ones that are fabricated by resentful church members can devastate a pastoral family without one shred of evidence or truth. It is little wonder that Revelation 12:10 refers to Satan as "the accuser of our brothers." The gospel affirms and commends us in truth, but the liar accuses and pulls down the pastor.

WHAT'S GOING ON HERE?

When you read about the violent reaction to New Testament pastors, you have to wonder, "What was really going on there?"

These were vagabond preachers with no reputation, no money, no education, no weapons and no tangible literature to distribute. They were men from the lower classes of life—fishermen, former tax collectors and labor-

7. LIST AT LEAST THREE THINGS YOU LEARNED FROM STUDYING THE EARLY CHURCH THAT YOU THINK MIGHT HELP YOU IN ESTABLISHING PRAYER FOR YOUR PASTOR.

1.

2.

3.

4.

ers. They preached a scandalous message about a convicted criminal who died on the cross by a garbage heap, saying that he was alive, having been raised from the dead, and that he was going to come back in the clouds to get those who believed in him! They claimed miracles in his name and said that he forgave sin. They even taught people to give to the poor and sell their property if necessary. How astounding!

Yet even more astounding was the reaction of the "officials" to this ragtag group of men. They put them in jail, beat them, exiled them and even killed them. Normally, the Jews and the Romans hated each other, but when it came to the Christians, they collaborated to get rid of them. In a world of constant religious debate and controversy, the Christians were always in the middle.

> *Normally, the Jews and the Romans hated each other, but when it came to the Christians, they collaborated to get rid of them.*

Were these few, itinerant preachers really a threat to undo the entire religious system of the day? Was their message of love and forgiveness putting lives at risk and national security on the line? What was really going on?

Paul had the answer in Ephesians 6:12:

> For our struggle is not against flesh and blood, but against the rulers, against the authorities, against the powers of this dark world and against the spiritual forces of evil in the heavenly realms.

These pastors faced resistance not just for political, economic or religious reasons. Rather, they were engaged in spiritual warfare. Behind the worldly scene of riots and angry religious officials were the unseen forces of Satan. The followers of Christ wanted to deliver captives into the kingdom of light. The forces of evil wanted to keep people locked up behind bars of empty religious rituals and false doctrine. The battle was for control. The question that was, and still is, being decided: "Who's in charge?"

Spiritual resistance to the gospel is not always an easy thing to nail down, but it is very real for most pastors today. Whether they are aware of it or not, they are still engaged in the same battle that started with Pentecost hundreds of years ago. It will not be over until Jesus returns and establishes his reign over the earth once and for all.

The battle for control in the spirit realm can be very subtle, as it is in the case of Jeff, a small church pastor in Vermont. Jeff told me that he dreads preaching his single Sunday morning service because of the incredible toll it takes on him physically:

> I go home, eat lunch, and fall in bed for three or four hours. When I wake up, I feel like I've been run over by a train. Preaching one sermon to 40 people just shouldn't be that hard. I used to love to preach, before I came to this church.

Jeff's situation is classic and much too common. Satan does not want people to be saved because transformed lives glorify God, and Satan hates that. He will promote and support anything that prevents people from understanding or accepting God's gift of eternal life.

C. Peter Wagner, in his book *Warfare Prayer*, writes:

> Jesus came to seek and save the lost. God sent his son that whosoever believes in him should have everlasting life. Whensoever a person is saved the angels in heaven rejoice. Satan hates all the above. He wants people to go to hell, not to heaven. And the reason this is his primary objective is that each time he succeeds he has won an eternal victory (61).

Let me share with you another story about spiritual warfare that, unlike Jeff's, was anything but subtle.

Years ago, Dr. Paul Walker, a very well-respected Church of God pastor, was flying back to his home in Atlanta. He sat next to a woman who refused the flight meal, saying, "No thank you. I'm fasting."

"Are you a Christian?" Dr. Walker asked the lady after the flight attendant moved on.

She replied, "No, I am a witch, and the covens of Atlanta are praying for the breakup of the marriages of some influential pastors." She named several, including Paul Walker.

> *Now there was a comforting thought! A group of dedicated, praying witches were literally hell-bent on tearing up his life.*

Now there was a comforting thought! A group of dedicated, praying witches were literally hell-bent on tearing up his life. That kind of resistance is pretty hard to ignore!

Although Jesus defeated Satan on the cross, for now, Satan still has permission to trip, destroy, meddle, hinder, and generally "haunt" efforts to preach the gospel. Territorial spirits fight constantly in whatever way possible to gain temporary control over lives and areas in order to prevent pastors and churches from winning the lost.

YESTERDAY, TODAY AND FOREVER

Clearly, it was not easy being a New Testament pastor. The perils of New Testament leadership were as real as the blessings.

The risks of pastoring today have not changed because the gospel has not changed. It is still the power of God unto the saving of souls. Neither has Jesus changed. He "is the same yesterday and today and forever" (Hebrews 13:8). So pastors today can expect to encounter the same kinds of trials and attacks as their early counterparts.

The gospel offers a new, better life in Christ. It calls people to holy living in a corrupt generation. It is a message of hope, forgiveness, love and grace. As the word goes forth, lives will be changed. New convictions will replace old, dead beliefs. Jesus will baptize people in new power and authority. New fruit will burst forth in churches.

But because we are in a spiritual conflict, as the kingdom grows, persecutions will follow. Everywhere the new order confronts the old order, there will be tension. Any pastor who preaches Jesus in all his fullness, majesty and truth will encounter opposition. As churches grow and become seekers of the lost, pastors will face all kinds of jealous accusations and threats from those who do not believe.

The enemy knows the principle in Zechariah 13:7, "Strike the shepherd, and the sheep will be scattered." If the pastor falters, the church has a difficult time. In all probability, when there is no life in the pulpit, there will be no life in the pew. No passion for souls in the pulpit means no passion for souls in the pew.

The pastor sets the pace and vision for the local congregation. Knowing this, the enemy's aim is to strike the pastor with fear, accusations, family problems, financial setbacks, sickness, disease, depression, fear of others, lawsuits and so on. You name it, and he will throw it at pastors' family relationships, their prayer lives, and their professional confidence. The enemy knows no detente. He is out to destroy pastors and their fruits.

A PERSONAL EXPERIENCE

Ironically, this book has always been surrounded by difficulty, illness, struggles and crises. During the original writing process, I experienced great resistance in the form of physical weakness and headaches. I en-

8. LIST AS MANY THINGS AS YOU CAN THINK OF THAT HAPPEN IN A COMMUNITY WHEN A PASTOR MAKES A VISIBLE, MORAL MISTAKE.

1.

2.

3.

4.

5.

6.

7.

8.

9.

10.

11.

12.

dured emotional attacks, depression, frustration and confusion. As I worked to complete the manuscript, my mother became ill and died. I had to ask for constant prayer from my church.

When I finally gave the manuscript to my typist, she got sick and was hampered with serious eye problems. I gave it to a second typist; and when I called her to pray for her protection, she was at the emergency room with her son. When the book was finally ready to print, the publishing company ran up against sudden financial setbacks, and the project was almost halted. Once on the press, the printer experienced technical difficulties that delayed the process further. When we decided to bring out this revised edition, we were faced with more of the same—illnesses, computer problems, unexpected distractions. It has become a joke among our staff, "What do you expect? It's *Preyed On or Prayed For.*"

AN URGENT CALL TO PRAY

A prayer hedge is urgent and necessary. If anyone grasps the importance of this message, it is Satan. This is one of the most serious issues facing the church today. As a layperson, you are the key to covering your shepherd in prayer, blessing and protecting him in ministry.

Your pastor is important in your life. She feeds you the word, teaches your children, gives you the sacraments and is with you in sorrow and death. Your pastor is there to represent Jesus Christ in your community.

Over the years, as I have interacted with pastors across our nation, I have observed one common thread that ties them all together. Peter Wagner sums it up when he states:

> Regardless of educational background, tenure, or denominational affiliation, relentless personal pressure is created from long hours of ministerial involvement in the lives of hurting and troubled people while at the same time being responsible for the disposition of their own family and the business of the church (*Shield* 66).

Without a personal prayer life, a strong hedge of protection and the blessing which comes through the intercession of the congregation, a pastor stands little chance of long-term success. In all probability, the hands of pastors who are not prayed for will grow too tired, they will fall to their sides and the battle will be lost.

It is imperative that we, the church, rise to the challenge and begin to hedge in our pastors with our prayers. Will you begin to raise up a prayer hedge in your church? Will you be the one to pray for your pastor like the early church did, with enough tenacity to save him from deadly peril? Will your pastor be preyed on or prayed for? It's up to you!

CHAPTER THREE

THE CHALLENGES ────────
Pastors Face

Tending to temperamental sheep while dealing with all the inherent perils of pastoring is difficult enough. But that's only part of the picture.

The institution of the church in this country today is in trouble. Many congregations are retreating, or worse yet, limping along in utter defeat. So far removed from their early church predecessors, they are suffering from confused identities, lack of vision, watered-down doctrine and a total absence of power and joy. According to a recent Focus on the Family survey, 3,000 to 4,000 of them are closing their doors every year (Ells).

The state of the church today is drastically affecting the well-being of pastors, and calls for an even more urgent mandate for prayer. In the same survey, Focus on the Family reported that approximately 1,500 pas-

1. WHY DO YOU THINK OVERALL CHURCH MEMBERSHIP, AND IN FACT, THE ACCEPTANCE OF CHRISTIAN IDEALS HAS DECLINED SO DRAMATICALLY IN RECENT YEARS?

HOW DO YOU THINK THIS MIGHT AFFECT YOUR PASTOR?

tors are leaving their assignments each month due to moral failure, spiritual burnout or contention within their congregation. Dr. Fred Gage of the Southern Baptist Church said in his book *Wounded Heroes* that 6,000 of that denomination's pastors leave the ministry each year, and 225 are fired each month (Ells). Bruce Grubbs of the Southern Baptist Sunday School Board reported that over an 18-month period that ended in 1989, more than 2,100 Southern Baptist ministers were dismissed, a 31 percent increase over a similar period that ended in 1985. Many factors are no doubt contributing to such dismal reports and the poor health of the church, but I will mention seven that I see firsthand week after week.

1. A Decline in Membership

The last several decades have seen an overall decline in church membership almost across the board in major protestant denominations. My own denomination, which recorded eleven million members in 1965, now has approximately eight million. That averages out to be a loss of about 85,000 members every year for 35 years! (General Board of Global Ministries) A 1998 Focus on the Family survey revealed that the number of people attending any kind of weekly religious activities in the United States has dropped off dramatically from 49 percent to 37 percent (Ells).

One of the reasons for the decline is that relatively few churches are experiencing any significant increase in membership as a result of new conversions. In other words, people are just not getting saved and joining churches. While some church rolls are increasing in number, others are decreasing—it isn't really church growth, it's just "sheep shifting." For example, in the United Methodist Church, about 80 percent of the local churches reported an increase in membership last year, but only 35 percent reported any professions of faith (General Board of Global Ministries). That means that over half of the churches that did grow did so because people left one church to join another. There is no net gain for Christianity in that, only redistribution.

> *Thousands of churches, tens of thousands of sermons preached, and not a single conversion. Not even one.*

What really bothers me, though, is how many worship services are represented by those numbers in which the church failed to accomplish its primary objective—to lead people to respond to the gospel of Jesus Christ. Thousands of churches, tens of thousands of sermons preached, and not a single conversion. Not even one.

2. Lame Worship

Let's face it—worship in many churches today is boring. Although there is a smorgasbord of great worship to be had, many churches choose not to partake. In these services, the music hasn't changed in 100 years, the litany for 200. The manifest presence of God is missing. The choir sings while the people watch, and the hymns are muttered with less passion than the Star-Spangled Banner at high school football games.

Worship like this is particularly unappealing to young people. I heard a motivational speaker claim that in 1970, teens felt that the church was the number one influence in their lives growing up. By 1980, it had dropped to number four. And in 1990, teens didn't even mention the church as an influence at all. Dry, dusty religion simply does not fill the need most people have today for spirituality that is real and relevant to daily life.

3. An absence of the Holy Spirit

The supernatural acts of the Holy Spirit, such as healing and deliverance, are often missing. We are ineffective when it comes to helping a society that is unraveling at the edges. We meet people with problems, and instead of being able to help, we simply act as a referral service. We plan weddings and conduct marriages, but we are unable to stem the tide of divorce right in our own families.

We are a church caught up on the natural, rationalistic, western view. Our loss of supernatural power leaves us limp in trying to stop abortion, domestic violence, teenage countercultures and child pornography.

We are so tame that people pass by our buildings on Sunday mornings without so much as a thought about what we are doing inside. Look around your community. Read the headlines; watch the news. The church has little discernible influence on anything that goes on around us. Pastors in a non-worshiping community feel tired rather than inspired.

4. Reliance on Marketing Techniques

Many churches have resorted to the latest marketing techniques to get a crowd. One church growth book after another simply states, "Find their need and meet it, and you will attract people." We offer thousands of programs and gimmicks to try and increase our membership, sometimes at the expense of true teaching and discipleship.

The sad result of this kind of approach is that we become very human-centered in all we do just to please people who might join. A human-centered gospel leaves out one important aspect—we the church are here to glorify God, not man. We have sold our bullets to buy a gun.

Pastors lose sight of their calling to confront sin when they are trying to make people "feel good" about themselves. They lose identity when they sell out to marketing skills rather than the Holy Spirit's leading and vision implantation.

5. High Levels of Conflict

Pastors today deal with conflict regularly, both in their own congregations and within their community of churches. A Fuller Institute study revealed that 40 percent of surveyed ministers had a serious conflict with

2. LIST SOME EXAMPLES YOU HAVE SEEN FIRST HAND OF "MARKETING TECHNIQUES" CHURCHES RELY ON TO ATTRACT PEOPLE.

1.

2.

3.

4.

5.

6.

ARE THEY EFFECTIVE? WHY OR WHY NOT?

someone in their church at least once a month, and 75 percent said they had a significant stress-related crisis at least once a month as well (Ells). *Leadership* magazine reported that of the ministers they asked, 25 percent had been fired or forced to resign at some point in their career, usually by a small group of people (ten or less) who had become unhappy (Ells). Pastoring requires advanced conflict resolution and people skills similar to those of a corporate CEO.

To compound the problems of conflict, most pastors feel isolated. When faced with a crisis, 70 percent say they have no close friends to turn to (Ells). Being on the defensive is draining for pastors, especially when they feel alone or at the mercy of a few.

Conflicts among pastors within a community are all too common as well. Instead of cooperating and blessing each other, many local church pastors become rivals, almost enemies, competing with each other for members and status. Sometimes the competition can become hurtful and damaging.

In addition, the church in America today is still racially divided. Although much progress is being made in some cities toward unity in the body of Christ, racism and denominationalism are very deeply rooted in some areas. We conduct our services, but we are unable to conduct a city-wide prayer service because of unwillingness to put aside minor differences and work together. We are not one in purpose and too often our goal is to build up our own camps with certificates of transfer. Pastors caught in parochial promotion often become the "kept-men" of an institution that exists for its tradition and name pride. The only motivation they have left is their pension program.

6. Moral Decline

The church as a whole is at a moral low. According to the Barna

Research Group, Christians today are more likely to experience divorce than are non-Christians (website). Holiness has given way to alternative life-styles, and church ruling bodies are being pressed to compromise positions on such issues as the ordination of homosexuals and the sanctity of human life.

When holiness and its definition are up for grabs, pastors lose their cutting edge. Fearful of being labeled "insensitive," they begin to tiptoe around issues lest they offend.

> *When holiness and its definition are up for grabs, pastors lose their cutting edge.*

One of the most tragic pastoral falls of our era involves the sexual abuse of children by Catholic priests. According to *Newsweek*, the molestation of children is "the worst clerical scandal in the modern history of the U.S. Catholic Church." The article states that allegations have been brought against approximately 400 priests since 1982, and that probably 2,500 other cases have gone unreported. To make the situation worse, the church was "slow to recognize the seriousness of its problem," and at times even went to great lengths to downplay or cover up the incidents (*Newsweek* 42-44). When such tragedies make headlines, all churches suffer in the pain and consequences.

7. Prayerlessness

Prayerlessness is a characteristic of many churches today. Many churches have no prayer room, no prayer coordinator, no prayer meetings, little prayer for the city and little or no prayer for the pastor. Seminaries are not teaching courses on prayer, and so pastors are not equipped or confident to train their people to pray. Often, prayer is seen only as a form of crisis management, and is not an integral part of church life. It is a "spare tire," so to speak, that gets pulled out in case of emergency.

A prayerless church is like a sailboat without sails. The Spirit's wind may be blowing, but there are no sails to catch it. Pastoring a prayerless church causes a pastor to depend on money and manpower to get the job done—neither of which are very effective in the spiritual realm. A pastor can burn out jumping from one promotional project to another in an effort to attract more people and keep the current ones happy.

HIGH EXPECTATIONS

Being the quarterback of a winning team can be fulfilling and exciting. However, being at the helm of a team with discouraging statistics is like facing third and long from your own end zone all the time. It could seem rather hopeless.

In addition to facing a difficult task, pastors today, like those in the book of Acts, also face a very real enemy. As the shepherds of the body of Christ and heralds of the gospel message, pastors are God's point men and women. That makes them Satan's number one target. When they lead the way into battle, they are the first to get fired at and they take the most direct hits. As a pastor to other pastors, I know this to be true.

Satan will do all he can to neutralize the effectiveness of an energetic pastor. The ones who have a passion for soul-winning are especially susceptible. Many of the scandals we hear about that involve influential pastors who have "fallen" are evidence of controlling spirits and darts of the enemy. Satan knows that pastors are vulnerable and he attacks them in their weakest moments. He knows that one good shot at the leader can bring a church to a screeching halt, throwing it into confusion for years.

Peter Wagner wisely observes:

We often fail to recognize the depth of the spiritual

battle we are fighting. The enemy knows pastors are beat up, he knows they are vulnerable, and he attacks them at their weakest point. This is not to say that these who have fallen are not themselves guilty and do not have character flaws that need to be repaired through humility, repentance, reconciliation, restoration and holiness. But I do hope and pray we will learn how to use our spiritual weapons more effectively in putting a stop to these blatant and all too successful attacks of the devil (*Shield* 66).

So against the backdrop of such discouraging circumstances, just what defines a successful ministry? What goes through the minds of pastors as they take stock of their own situations?

3. DISCUSS BARNA'S LIST OF EXPECTATIONS. DO PASTORS HAVE A REALISTIC VIEW OF WHAT IS EXPECTED OF THEM?

HOW WOULD YOUR LIST BE DIFFERENT?

What do they think that you, their congregations, want them to be?

According to George Barna, here is what pastors think their people expect of them:

1.   Live an exemplary life.

2.   Be available at all times to all people for all purposes.

3.   Lead the church to grow numerically.

4.   Balance wisdom with leadership and love.

5.   Teach people the deeper truths of the faith in ways that are readily applicable in all life situations.

6.   Be committed to your family and demonstrate spiritual leadership in your family; love your spouse and provide a positive role model for children.

7.   Keep pace with the latest trends and developments of church life.

8.   Build significant relationships with members of the congregation.

9.   Represent the church in the community.

10. Grow spiritually.

11. Run the church in a crisp, professional, businesslike manner without taking on a cold, calculating air (*Pastors* 52).

Wow! Read the list again. Do you realize that to fulfill such expectations, a person would have to be highly organized, yet spontaneous, practical yet visionary, administrative yet relational, and disciplined yet flexible. And of course, they have to be willing to make great sacrifices in their personal lives and do it all for a menial salary, because after all, it's ministry!

When you think about it, it is not hard to understand why hundreds of pastors every month throw up their hands in despair and walk away from their pulpits. The circumstances are challenging at best, and the pressure can be fierce and unrelenting. In many cases, morale is at an all time low, and progress or change seem unattainable.

MUSEUM DUTY

Some time ago, my wife and I toured the U.S.S. Lexington. Now in permanent dock in Corpus Christi, Texas, this mammoth aircraft carrier saw more action during its half century tenure than any other American warship. Today it is a floating museum of war relics and memories.

The youthful crew, few of whom have ever seen combat, simply show photos and movies of the once-proud ship's "glory days" to hundreds of tourists who tramp up and down its steel-plated decks each day. The war planes are bolted down, engines lifeless. The combat information room is silent. Places that not long ago hummed with the activity of thousands of young men in full battle alert are now deadly still. A heavily armored room that once served as the storehouse for tons of ammunition is now a tastefully decorated coffee shop. The crew of the Lexington still *looks* polished and ready for battle, but their only responsibilities now are to give tours, pour coffee and entertain people with stories of past exploits.

> ...*I thought of many pastors today...who simulate something that is unreal and irrelevant to families being torn apart....*

As I stood on the upper deck, my hands grasping the rail, my heart swelled with the realization that the fate of our country once rested in this and a half-dozen other carriers. And, as I turned to leave, I felt a ghostly sense of sadness at the thought of this once powerful, military vessel that now sat idle, never again to do what it was created to do.

As we were being led through the tour, I thought of many pastors today who are much like the present crew of the Lexington—pastors who hold up pictures of past captains and tell of their missions, pastors who show the war reels of victory, only to see defeat in the eyes of their parishioners, pastors today who simulate something that is unreal and irrelevant to families being torn apart, and pastors who get the mail, order the candles, mow the grass and try to keep everybody happy.

How sad it is that these modern day pastors have been taken off the front lines, stripped of the supernatural, toned down and left with little passion for lost souls. How unfortunate it is to see pastors using modern marketing techniques to get the crowd in for a head count. How tragic is the identity crisis in preaching that drives pastors to flip through the latest book looking for a sermon.

> *Pastors are frustrated because they signed up to serve on a battleship, but got museum duty instead!*

No wonder pastors are burned out! They are tired of talking about what was and only imagining what could be. Pastors are frustrated because they signed up to serve on a battleship, but got museum duty instead! Many pastors would love to turn things around, but their efforts are useless without the support of the laity.

A few years ago I preached at a church in New York. As I spoke, I noticed that the organist was reading a magazine! During my entire sermon, I never once saw her look up. I later found out that she had become angry because of some changes that had taken place in the church and her method of retaliation was to ignore anyone who set foot in the pulpit! The most tragic thing about the situation was that the laity would not support the pastor's efforts to remove her.

Because of the church's state of affairs, many pastors are taking it on the chin—getting blamed for the team's poor performance. No wonder hundreds of pastors are discarded every month because they don't produce. In some respects, the church has had too many losing seasons in a row.

Pastors are hard pressed. Instead of managing revival, they often spend valuable time managing the flock's divorces and petty complaints. Anyone who has been pastoring for several years has probably had plenty of visits or phone calls from angry members saying, "I wanted to be on the finance committee" or "Someone moved our table in the foyer" or "My daughter didn't get a part in the Christmas play!" My favorite was, "You didn't pray for me this morning at the altar. Why don't you like me?" The pastor of an East Texas church felt led to let a teen lead the praise service one Sunday night. The official song leader got so angry because he hadn't been consulted first that he left the church. The pastor had to beg him to come back.

It is little wonder that pastors retire on the inside at 35 and jump overboard in personal or professional crises. One denomination has a room with files stacked to the ceiling of defrocked

4. WHAT FACTORS MIGHT KEEP A CHURCH LIVING IN THE PAST, AS SUGGESTED BY "MUSEUM DUTY"?

5. HOW DID THE INFORMATION IN THIS CHAPTER BETTER EQUIP YOU TO PRAY FOR YOUR SHEPHERD?

ministers. I talked to the secretary of that room who handles ministerial credentials, and he just wept as he told me of the most recent file added—his own pastor. This leadership crisis is a sad contrast to the bold, almost reckless determination that characterized pastors in the book of Acts. The call to pray for our pastors in a new and bold manner is urgent if we are to break out of the cocoon of religious doldrums.

As we look at the current state of the church, we can hear the Lord's plea in Ezekiel 22:30, "I looked for a man among them who would build up the wall and stand before me in the gap on behalf of the land so I would not have to destroy it, but I found none."

Will the Lord find any to stand in the gap and restore the prayer hedge for shepherds today? Much more is in jeopardy than just the personal lives of pastors and their marriages. The future of the church in America is at stake. The church's ability to be that redemptive, powerful, chosen nation of God to proclaim Jesus Christ to every nation is on the line.

We are like a great warship, sailing into enemy waters to free the captives and undo the works of Satan. But we need pastors who are fully alive in Christ to lead the way. If there is no fire in the pulpit, there will be no fire in the pew. If the pastor has no vision, board meetings will be visionless and boring as well. If the pastor does not have a passion for lost souls, certainly the laity won't either. The church may have a board of elders, but there must be a leader among leaders to set the pace and sound the trumpet.

Every year at our annual conference, I am deeply troubled by what I see in the book room. Worn out, desperate ministers circle the book table thinking, "Maybe this new book on church growth will be the answer. If I can just find out about the latest techniques. I'm sure my church will flourish!" Unfortunately, this approach will never work.

What we really need is a new and fresh outpouring of the Holy Spirit, not just a new technique. I'm not speaking of some short-lived charismatic movement, but rather the supernatural impetus of Acts chapters 1-28. We need a baptism of the Spirit to anoint and empower pastors to enter into a whole new dimension of preaching and leading! I believe the hope for this divine outpouring will be prayer hedges beseeching God in behalf of their pastors.

CHAPTER FOUR

PREYED ON OR _____
Prayed For

"Minister Resigns Over Misconduct 'Long Ago'."

That bold headline stared at Rev. David from the front page of his local newspaper. It had to be one of the most heartbreaking moments of his life.

One of the city's highest profile pastors was asked to resign from his once-thriving church. The action was taken following allegations that he had an affair five years before with a woman he was counseling, and had been involved with four other affairs earlier in his ministry.

A laywoman said the 3,000-member church had become "painfully divided" over the issue. "It split the church," she explained.

"His supporters wanted to fight his firing," a former parishioner reported. "They believed David was the victim of a small group of reli-

1. PASTORS ARE OFTEN REFERRED TO AS "SHEPHERDS." WHAT DOES THIS INFER ABOUT THEIR RELATIONSHIP TO THEIR "FLOCKS?"

2. SHOULD PASTORS BE DISCREDITED FOR MISTAKES IN THEIR PAST? SUPPORT YOUR ANSWER WITH AN EXAMPLE FROM SCRIPTURE.

gious zealots who were incapable of forgiving his previous indiscretions." Whether or not David was the victim of a "witch hunt," as one member called the probe, was never determined.

Those who wanted the minister terminated immediately pointed to the 300 to 500 members who stopped worshiping because of the turmoil. "The trust was broken," an opponent of the pastor said. "He had to go!"

Incidents like this one happen with regrettable regularity. In just one week, I learned of several similar tragedies. On Monday, one of Oklahoma's promising young pastors informed me that he had AIDS. Tuesday afternoon, a newly married pastor from Indiana told me his bride had admitted to being a lesbian. Thursday, I received a letter from a pastor whose admission of sin made me cry. And on Friday, I opened the newspaper to find an article about a priest from Chicago who was being charged with molesting more than a dozen young boys.

As I have said before, Satan hates pastors. He keeps them under attack on every side in every way he can. He exploits their weaknesses and then preys on their mistakes. As one retired minister from Kansas City professed, "All pastors have their human frailties. Some have problems with alcohol, others seem to attract women like magnets. And then there are those who blatantly plagiarize other preachers' sermons so they can slip away for golf or worse. I've never met a pastor who wasn't having a problem in some area of his life."

A friend said to me several years ago just after the Gulf War ended that "modern pastorates look like the road from Kuwait to Baghdad—burned out and abandoned."

As I travel from city to city, I meet dozens of pastors every month. It deeply troubles me how many of them feel used and blown to bits, having lost the fire and boldness that carried them through seminary. Some can be piled together as moral failures, unable to move because they are bogged down in guilt and shame. Others feel lost with no direction and a deep sense of fear. Many are troubled by a loss of identity or a lack of support from denominational headquarters. They lack the confidence to move in any direction. It is painful to see.

Pastors who once preached with passion have surrendered to the forces of evil and now, herding with others who have fallen from grace, often lament their problems and talk with disdain about fellow pastors who have not erred—or have not been caught in their indiscretions. C. Peter Wagner is right when he notes:

> In a word—pastors need help—at least more help than they have been getting. In the course of a year, I meet and interact with hundreds of pastors. Even though I do not relate to them as a counselor or as pastor to pastor, I find that many are beaten up spiritually, emotionally, and sometimes physically (*Shield* 63).

Why is the highway littered with defeat and spiritual death? Could it be that we take our pastors for granted and shoot them instead of praying for them? If this is the case, I wonder if it is too late for us to repent for our lack of prayer for our shepherds and bear the fruits of repentance in a new zeal to pray for them.

> *Could it be that we take our pastors for granted and shoot them instead of praying for them?*

Exodus 17 gives us a powerful and very literal model of what pastoral support looks like. It is the passage that much of this book is based on. In it, Pastor Moses was having a hard time. At Rephidim, the Israelites were short on water and they blamed Moses, their leader. The people called a meeting of the B.T.E. (Back to Egypt) Committee to grumble against him and generally carve him up because of their troubles. When he heard about their meeting, Moses was frustrated, and asked the Lord, "What am I to do with these people? They are almost ready to stone me." So the Lord came to his rescue, provided water, and the B.T.E. Committee adjourned.

Moses probably thought his troubles were over. But just as everyone settled down, the Amalekites attacked. Moses ordered Joshua into battle and took Aaron and Hur to the top of the hill to pray. As he watched the battle, he lifted his hands over the people. We read, "As long as Moses held up his hands, the Israelites were winning, but whenever he lowered his hands, the Amalekites were winning" (Exodus 17:11).

As the battle dragged on, Aaron and Hur noticed that Moses' hands were growing tired, and they quickly discerned the danger this might cause the Israelites. So Aaron and Hur found a large stone and sat their pastor on it between them. With one on one side and one on the other, they held up his weary arms so that Moses' hands "remained steady until sunset"

(Exodus 17:12). The end result was a victory for the people of God. What a beautiful demonstration of support for a tired, battle-worn pastor!

Although you will probably never have an occasion to physically support your pastor's arms, the picture of Moses, Aaron and Hur on the hill is a symbolic expression of what happens when you pray for your pastor. On one side, pastors need prayer protection for themselves and their families. We are battling the enemy who comes "only to steal and kill and destroy" (John 10:10). He preys on pastors with an arsenal of destructive forces.

On the other side, since pastors do spiritual work, they need prayer for spiritual anointing and blessing. In your prayers, you can ask God to make your pastor fruitful. Jesus told his disciples in John 15:7-8, "...ask whatever you wish, and it will be given you. This is to my Father's glory, that you bear much fruit...." The Holy Spirit honors prayers for pastors by blessing their work, both preaching and soul-winning.

> *...prayers of protection and prayers of blessing—together they result in victory for your pastor and for the ultimate purpose of God.*

Aaron and Hur—prayers of protection and prayers of blessing—together they result in victory for your pastor and for the ultimate purpose of God.

Your pastor needs your support— more than just dashing off a few prayer phrases once in a while on his behalf. By prayer support, I am talking about a hedge of people recruited, planted, trained, aimed and motivated to consistently pray for the pastor. As a layperson, you are responsible for making this happen.

THREE AREAS OF VULNERABILITY

"Some members may fall asleep when I'm preaching on Sunday

morning, but you can bet they keep 'one eye open' to see how I live my life the rest of the week."

That's the sentiment of a minister who transgressed once too often and was caught. Now he feels the close scrutiny of his 1,250-member church in southern California. "Living the life of a pastor is a mine field," he said. "Ever since the Jimmy Swaggart and Jim Bakker scandals, every preacher in the country has ended up on someone's 'watch list.'"

Pastors need to be prayed for, not preyed on! The rest of this chapter is devoted to showing you more specifically, through real-life examples, the three main areas of your pastor's life that need to be hedged in. Based on what pastors have told me are their greatest needs, I want to help you understand where they feel your prayers can ease their burdens the most.

The purpose of the following stories is not to condemn the people involved in any way, nor to sensationalize their personal tragedies, but to raise your level of awareness about what pastors and their families go through. The more you understand about the realities of pastoral life, the more compassionate and discerning you can be as you pray for your own shepherd.

The three areas in your pastor's life and ministry that are most likely to come under attack are his (1) personal life (2) prayer life and (3) professional life.

Personal Life

Meet Frank. He's ministering to the people served by a 3-point charge in rural New Mexico, and he is a good pastor. In order to remain readily available to his far-flung flock, Frank wears a beeper on his belt and carries a cellular phone in his attache. When he is not preaching a sermon, ministering to the sick, recruiting new members, handling the maintenance of his three churches or performing any of the 101 other duties of a pastor, Frank is riding in a patrol car talking to the officers he serves as a police chaplain. Last month, he launched a 12-step recovery program for drug addicts.

What's the problem?

Big-hearted Frank has no life of his own. He is always on call. His private life is suffering, and his wife is hooked on over-the-counter medications for her frayed nerves. "I love Frank," she says, "but I hate the strain his duties are placing on our marriage. Even during our most intimate moments, I have to worry about the phone ringing or his beeper going off."

Frank and his wife aren't alone. At a small church in upstate New York, the pastor's wife is boiling mad about having to live in a parsonage with a side door that leads right into the church. "People treat our home like it is the church's fellowship hall," she says. "They think nothing of raiding our kitchen for whatever supplies and utensils are needed for Wednesday night dinners."

To add insult to injury, the pastor's wife is expected to attend all

3. READ EXODUS 17:8-16. WHAT DOES THIS PASSAGE TELL YOU ABOUT GOD'S RELATIONSHIP TO PASTOR MOSES?

4. SHOULD PASTORS BE MORE ACCOUNTABLE FOR THEIR PERSONAL LIVES THAN LAYPEOPLE BECAUSE OF THEIR LEADERSHIP ROLE?

of the women's functions. "When I'm five minutes late, someone sticks her head in our side door and hollers, 'Shirley, are you coming to our meeting?' What is expected of a pastor's wife is unreal."

> *When all hell is breaking loose in the parsonage, it's hard to stand up on Sunday morning and be full of the joy of the Lord.*

According to one survey, 80 percent of pastors say their family life has been negatively affected as a result of their current ministry while 33 percent say that being in ministry is "an outright hazard" (Ells). Another survey reported that 49 percent admitted that their family life had "suffered significantly" as a result of ministry (Ells). When Focus on the Family surveyed pastors and their spouses, 84 percent described themselves as being discouraged or in depression (Ells).

In a survey conducted by *Spice*, a newsletter for wives of ministers, one respondent wrote that "by the time my pastor-husband gets through unloading all of his own problems and the problems of his members on me, he's too tired to listen to my problems." Then, without signing her name, she added the following postscript: "I am having an affair with our organist. He's old enough to be my father, but at least he listens to me and makes me feel like I am the most important person in his life!"

Adults aren't the only ones who suffer. Children of pastors have a common complaint that the church always takes precedence over their needs. "My dad's a great guy," the daughter of a pastor in Salem, Oregon says. "I just wish he would give me some of the attention he gives his parishioners."

Most people, even pastors, find work a difficult place to be when things aren't going well at home. George Barna interviewed a 12-year veteran pastor who admitted, "Sometimes I feel ashamed to go to church on Sunday because of how our family is struggling" (*Pastors* 61-62). When all hell is breaking loose in the parsonage, it's hard to stand up on Sunday morning and be full of the joy of the Lord.

It is easy to forget that pastors are only human, and that they also have to deal with all of the problems that go along with living in a fallen world. We are all vulnerable to personal attacks against ourselves and our families.

When their personal lives are under fire, pastors lose confidence and begin to retreat. The boldness they need to proclaim the gospel is dulled by the fear of "friendly fire" against themselves or their families. A pastor cannot effectively fight the world while fearing for the well-being of those he loves.

It is almost impossible to take aim at someone you are earnestly lifting up in prayer. Therefore, the more people you recruit in your church to pray for your pastor, the fewer will be left to join the firing squad! Prayer hedges help create an atmosphere of appreciation and love for the pastor and his family, and will help free him to do the work of ministry.

> *...the more people you recruit in your church to pray for your pastor, the fewer will be left to join the firing squad!*

Prayer Life

Say "hello" to Ray. He is the 27-year-old pastor of a historic little church in the southernmost foothills of the Appalachian mountains. After lunch last Saturday, Ray went to the community funeral home to comfort the family of one of his closest friends and his most outspoken supporter. For Ray, this church member's death was a very personal loss. As he embraced the widow and her two young sons to pray, tears streamed down his cheeks. The young pastor felt drained as he left the mourners

5. WHEN DOES YOUR PASTOR
WORSHIP? WHEN DOES HE HAVE
TIME ALONE TO PRAY?

6. HOW COULD YOU ENCOURAGE
YOUR PASTOR'S ONGOING SPIRITUAL
RENEWAL?

behind and hurried to the nearest flo-
rist to pick up flowers that had been
ordered to decorate the church for a
wedding that evening.

At 7:00 p.m., he stood in front
of a deliriously happy young couple and
performed their wedding ceremony.
Following the reception, Ray immediately went to his study. There he spent
an hour polishing the sermon he would
preach the following morning, and two
hours preparing the eulogy he would
deliver on Monday.

For Ray and other pastors, life is
an emotional roller coaster. Because
ministers are usually in contact with
dozens of members every day, it is not
unusual for them to deal with all points
on the emotion spectrum in a short
time. Comforting the grieving, reassur-
ing the anxious and rejoicing with the
joyful can be all in a day's work. Sometimes the swings from one appointment
to the next can be dramatic, a dynamic
that can be emotionally and spiritually
draining for even the most energetic
shepherds.

That is why worship and praise
are so important for pastors. Worship

fills their cups, and praise revives them emotionally. Pastors thrive on good worship!

But when do pastors worship God? They lead us in worship, yet when they step into the pulpit, they have a great deal more on their minds than simply delivering the sermon.

Chances are, your pastor has to think about the thermostat, a shortage of workers in the nursery, spotting any special guests, remembering all of the announcements, and a lot of other non-worship concerns. Of course, in the midst of it all, your pastor is trying to stay tuned-in to the expressions on the faces of the worshipers and to what the Holy Spirit may be saying during the worship service.

Could it be that the pastor worships less than any other person at the service? If this is the case, your pastor's spiritual and emotional cup may not be getting filled. Her hands may be growing weary and falling to the side. She may feel depressed or burned out when she is deprived of good, intimate, exalted corporate and private worship.

How about your pastor's prayer life? Just as the emotional roller coaster may rob your pastor of good praise time, "busyness" can steal away the average pastor's prayer life.

According to a former pastor who is now president of a church college, "a pastor lives in a 'pressure cooker' of unrealistic expectations." After pausing a moment, he adds, "Listen to what a pastor says when one of his members approaches him. The pastor will invariably feel compelled to say something to justify what he is doing at the moment. For example, if he is having lunch with a layman, and another church member comes over to their table, the pastor will say, 'Just having lunch with one of our finest members,' or something to that effect."

A pastor from Michigan agreed. "It's a sad commentary, but we pastors stay constantly busy trying to live up to someone else's expectations."

Most pastors desire stronger prayer lives, yet the average time spent in prayer among evangelical pastors according to one national poll is only seven minutes a day. C. Peter Wagner did a survey of 572 American pastors across regional, age and denominational lines. He found that 57 percent pray less than 20 minutes a day, 34 percent pray between 20 minutes and one hour a day, and 9 percent pray one hour or more a day. The average prayer time according to his survey was 22 minutes per day. He also found that 28 percent, or approximately 1 out of 4, pray less than 10 minutes a day! (*Shield* 78-79)

The desire to pray is preyed on by church administration, budget matters, visitation, public relations, church maintenance, endless committee meetings and various practical services like giving Sister Jones a ride to church. Sometimes the telephone can become the worst enemy of a pastor's strong, consistent prayer life. In addition, pastors, like others, are subject to laziness, impatience, rebelliousness and unconfessed sin.

Yet, "busyness" is no new problem, for the early church also had to deal with overwhelming demands in its beginning. The first five chapters of Acts report an estimated 20,000 conversions! In Acts 6, the apostles elected deacons to help serve the people so they could devote themselves to prayer and ministry. They knew how to delegate.

As you know, your pastor is a professional, but what he does is spiritual. He evangelizes the lost, teaches about God, prays for the sick and counsels the wounded. Since all ministry is rooted in the Holy Spirit, the pastor needs the Spirit's anointing to present Jesus with power and authority.

A pastor who takes the time to praise God and pray in the Holy Spirit is built up and blessed spiritually and emotionally. Jude wrote, "But you, dear friends, build yourselves up in your most holy faith and pray in the Holy Spirit" (verse 20). On several occasions in Luke, when Jesus prayed, the Spirit came on him also. We read in Luke 3:21-22, "...as he was praying, heaven was opened and the Holy Spirit descended on him in bodily form like a dove." In Acts 2, while the apostles were praying continually, the Spirit came upon them as well. We receive the Holy Spirit when we pray, and more important, the Spirit receives us.

> *We receive the Holy Spirit when we pray, and more important, the Spirit receives us.*

Your pastor needs to be refreshed through prayer and praise daily, especially when she is being stretched beyond human limits to minister, counsel and care for the flock.

Your pastor needs your help!

One of the most critical elements of any successful ministry is the pastor's own spiritual life. A pastor who is too busy to spend time alone with God is headed for trouble. If the enemy can keep a pastor too burdened to make a joyful noise in praise, or keep that pastor out of the prayer closet, then he can cut the pastor off from the vital source, and the anointing that pastor needs to present Jesus to the world.

Consider a pastor named Caroline. She is a devoted pastor who rises early to spend time with God, spending two hours each morning in prayer. She preaches on prayer and calls her church to pray for the lost. She is always looking for ways to motivate her people to pray for their city to be taken for God. Because she truly desires to hear from God, one day a week she fasts for her sermon preparation.

Caroline's church is rapidly outgrowing its building, which seats 300. It is packed for both worship services. Five to ten new families are visiting each week. As the church is growing, hurting people are being at-

7. IF CAROLINE WAS YOUR PASTOR, WHAT STEPS COULD YOU TAKE TO KEEP HER BLESSED AND PROTECTED?

tracted, many of whom need or want to be counseled by Caroline personally. She is doing more and more, and staying up later and later to return phone calls. She is finding it harder to get up in the morning. In a growing church, everybody wants something from her—her time, her prayers, her presence or her advice.

Slowly, the demands of her growing church begin to eat away at Caroline's two-hour morning prayer sessions, and she finds herself praying less and less. Pastor Caroline's hands are not as high as they used to be. And to add to her growing frustration, she is plagued by the tyranny of the unfinished because every day more and more is left undone.

The pressure on your pastor, as on Pastor Caroline, can build to unreal proportions, especially if your church is growing. Most believe it is a privilege to lead God's people into a deeper relationship with him. More frequently than not, however, the privilege fits around the pastor's neck like a noose. It is only by the grace of God," the pastor reasons, "the slack in the rope has not been tightened" (Barna, *Pastors* 52).

As a layperson, you can stand in the gap for your pastor's spiritual life to make sure that the enemy does not rob him of vital worship and prayer time. As believers, we all have authority and power in Jesus' name to stand against any of the enemy's assignments, and to build up a hedge of protection around those we pray for.

Does anyone in your church support your pastor in this way, or is everyone too busy trying to get what they can from him? Do the deacons encourage your pastor to take time away and pray? Does your Board insist that she take a week every year to go on a retreat to seek God?

Perhaps you can instigate some of these thoughts. Not only will your pastor be grateful and encouraged, but you will begin to see the results in the life of your church as the Spirit enables your pastor and fills his cup.

Professional Life

A family man in his late forties, Don was the pastor of a newly-constructed church on the outskirts of a city in Florida. The upper middle-class neighborhood that surrounded the church was sprinkled with back-yard swimming pools and community parks. Across the street from the church, a large, upscale retail complex was nearing completion. His wife loved the area and his two children were doing well in school.

Then one day things began to crumble for Don when five of the church's leading laymen asked him to join them for lunch. Halfway through the meal, the group's self-appointed spokesman cleared his throat and began, "Pastor, we are deeply concerned about our church's lack of growth. We know you had a vision, and you've tried a number of approaches. But quite frankly, they aren't working. The Baptist church is growing by leaps and bounds, and our church isn't." Don shifted uneasily in his chair as the spokesman continued. "We love you, and we want the best for you. We

8. WHEN A CHURCH IS OBVIOUSLY "LOSING GROUND," WHO IS RESPONSIBLE? WHAT WOULD BE A SCRIPTURAL COURSE OF ACTION?

9. WHEN, IF EVER, WOULD IT BE APPROPRIATE FOR A TEAM OF LEADERS TO "CONFRONT" THEIR SHEPHERD?

told you that when we hired you. But, we've got to start thinking about what's best for our church."

Don's stomach was tied in knots as he drove home, deeply hurt and frustrated. His head spun. *What should I do? Should I go or stay? How can I tell my daughter that she may have to transfer during her senior year of high school? What will my wife say if she has to quit her job and pack up for another move? Lord, what am I to do?*

When things aren't going as expected in a church, usually the pastor gets blamed.

Satan can use well-meaning but insensitive people and the circumstances surrounding a pastor's life to try and throw him off the course that God has set. When a pastor wants to try something new, the old-timers often resist change by digging in their heels. For example, a pastor in Indiana told me about a man in her church who would get up and walk out of the sanctuary the moment she started to preach. Resisting change provided him the attention he was looking for. In one of the first churches I pastored, when I stepped into the pulpit, a woman who invariably sat in the front pew would actually place her fingers in her ears to avoid hearing me preach! That is persistent resistance.

Since the working life of a pastor is the most visible to his congregations and to his peers, it is often the most attacked area. The enemy can shoot darts at your pastor's professional life through other preachers or political forces. He can attack your pastor's preaching life with deceptive distractions or through unhappy factions in the church. And he loves to wear down your pastor as he perseveres through the obstacle course of ministry.

Quite often, pastors' professional lives can come under attack from all sides, and even their own peers can become a force against them. For example, most pastors get saturated with ideas from those who are considered successful in ministry, creating "information overloads." Also, pastors can face political forces and competition within their denominations. Preachers' meetings can be depressing when the numbers game or salary ladder is the chief source of conversation.

Frequently, pastors feel intimidated or frustrated by power groups in their churches. It is amazing how a small group of four or five "godly" men and women can devour a pastor and his entire family! One man in a small town in Ohio appointed himself to his church's welcoming committee, and would greet visitors by asking them to go back to where they came from.

> *It is amazing how a small group of four or five "godly" men and women can devour a pastor and his entire family!*

Let me give you another example of a pastor whose professional life seems to be the enemy's target—pastor Chris. He loves to preach and considers this his highest calling as a pastor. He believes in the power of the spoken word to convict, convince and bring people to salvation, and he is deeply convinced that the word of God inspires, rebukes, heals and conforms the church to the image of God in Jesus Christ. He seeks God for messages that speak to his church's heart, vision and mission. He also tries to interpret the times to his people when in the pulpit, so he wants to be prayed up and read up. As a shepherd, he strives to have a good feel of where his flock is.

The church Chris pastors is growing and attracting new members from the outskirts of the city, despite its downtown location. It now has over 3,000 on the rolls with a staff of 16 full-time employees. They are worshiping four services during the week, three on Sunday and one on Wednesday night. Many of the outreach programs of the church are doing well, and because of the church's size and influence, Chris is being called on more and more to take the lead in city-wide ministry efforts that involve other churches. In addition, churches in his own denomination call regularly asking him to come teach and preach. As Chris's staff looks to the future with high expectations, his board of deacons are working on purchasing land on the edge of town so the church can move closer to the areas of growth.

So why does Chris desperately need prayer? The demands on Chris's time are starting to encroach on his valuable preparation time. His passion for preaching and his dedication to always deliver a powerful, fresh word are being frustrated by all the pressures. In between meetings, counseling sessions, administrative duties, and more meetings, Chris is finding it almost impossible to study and prepare like he wants to. He can't cut into what little family time he has with his three children, but he knows that something has to give. Now in his thirteenth year, the pressure to come up with new material and maintain his track record as a leader among his peers is getting to him. Although no one can tell, this pastor feels his hands growing tired.

According to Barna, just over 70 percent of the pastors he surveyed said that either preaching, teaching or discipling people is their primary source of joy in the ministry. But with all the other demands on their time, it is difficult for many to feel adequately prepared. He found that 77 percent of senior pastors spend at least 6 hours per week preparing sermons, and many of those spend well over 10 hours. Barna states, "Ministry is tough work, and thousands of pastors bear the scars to prove it. Although many lay members idealize the work of the clergy, the harsh reality is that despite the best efforts of these learned individuals and regardless of the high and holy nature of the calling, pastoring a church is more burdensome than most people realize" (*Pastors* 63-65).

As I mentioned in chapter three, hundreds of pastors are released each month by dissatisfied congregations who need someone to blame. Hundreds more simply burn out and quietly leave the ministry for good. When their professional lives come under heavy fire, or begin to do irreparable damage to their personal lives, many pastors lose

> *...hundreds of pastors are released each month by dissatisfied congregations who need someone to blame.*

their zeal for spiritual work and retreat to the safety of a "normal" life.

Finally, let me introduce you to Paul, whose situation is all too common among seasoned preachers. After 30 years in the ministry, Paul is tired. Although pastoring has been fulfilling, he is now 54 years old, and dreams of retiring and doing something else. His wife suspects that he has chronic fatigue syndrome because he feels deeply tired all the time. The free time he used to spend pursuing outdoor hobbies is now spent at home in front of the television. Regardless of what he does, he cannot seem to recover or feel rested.

Because of his constant exhaustion, his confidence has diminished,

10. LIST SOME SPECIFIC PRAYER POINTS FOR YOUR PASTOR UNDER EACH HEADING.

PERSONAL LIFE

1.

2.

3.

PRAYER LIFE

1.

2.

3.

PROFESSIONAL LIFE

1.

2.

3.

and his only goal is to keep people in the church happy and avoid any kind of crisis. When he gets a letter, he is afraid it might be critical, and another church controversy is just more than he could stand. The wounds he bears from past skirmishes and friendly fire are still painful.

Although Paul dreams of doing something else, his church pension plan means everything to him, so he is afraid to say anything. Feeling lonely and paranoid, he just wants to get by.

The results of Paul's condition are not hard to predict. He will have a difficult time leading a congregation in dynamic, "early church" ministry. He will choose mediocrity over excellence in order to maintain the status quo. His fear of crises will make him extremely vulnerable to church controllers and skeptical of anything new or different.

Pastors like Chris and Paul need a prayer covering to support and strengthen their professional lives. They need to be receiving a steady stream of prayer for courage, energy, wisdom and vision. They need prayers of encouragement and protection that will enable them to persevere in spite of hardships. They need the power of the Holy Spirit to fulfill God's purpose for them.

As a layperson you can pray for your pastor's professional standing, reputation, success as a shepherd and relationship to the flock. You can pray that God grant your pastor a bold vision, and that this vision will be blessed and accepted in the church. Her sermons will only be as good as the prayer force behind them. You can pray for your pastor to have a deep sense of peace and fulfillment, as well as the perseverance to finish the race. Help plant a prayer hedge around your pastor that will keep him feeling refired, and not retired.

CHAPTER FIVE

ESTABLISHING A ────────
Prayer Hedge

William Carey was a soft-spoken, deeply conscientious shoe repairman who lived in England at the turn of the century. Patrons arrived at his modest shop in horse-drawn carriages. As he hammered on new heels, cut and glued leather, and replaced worn shoe laces, his thoughts frequently wandered to a map of the world that he had tacked above his workbench.

William was a unique man. He wasn't dreaming of seeing far away lands or taking exotic trips. His concern was for people—more specifically, souls. "Who is going to carry the good news of Jesus Christ to the unsaved millions who live in all those far-off countries?" he wondered. "How are they going to know?" In the evenings, he would often ask his crippled sister the same question, "Who is going to go?"

Then one morning, as William prayed, God answered, "You! I want you to go share the gospel to those who have never heard."

The cobbler packed up his belongings, caught a steamer and followed the needle on his compass to India, where he labored for 42 years. Today, Carey and his co-workers are best remembered for having translated the Bible into 26 Indian languages and the New Testament into 25 more. Carey has been credited with leading millions to accept Jesus Christ as Lord and Savior—and for inspiring countless hundreds of young men and women around the globe to become missionaries.

But there's a key part of the story that sometimes gets overlooked. At least once a week, Carey wrote to his frail, bedridden sister asking her to pray for divine guidance in his efforts. Hour after hour, week after week, year after year, she kept her brother and his work before the Lord. She was the "secret force" behind his ministry.

Within every church there are persons who, if asked, will become praying saints for your pastor. They may be shut-ins, youth, nursing home residents or prisoners. Some will be experienced prayer warriors and others will be brand new Christians. Chances are, some of your most active members will be honored to become intercessors in behalf of your pastor if given the opportunity.

You may be asking yourself at this point, "Where do I begin? I understand this is important and I want to help my pastor. I like the idea of a prayer hedge, but I'm not sure how to start."

My goal in this chapter is to give you some practical information you need to begin to organize a prayer force for your shepherd.

PLANTING THE HEDGE

1. Get Organized With a Plan

If you have ever been a part of a church that was involved in a building program, then you probably know just how organized and intentional a determined church body can be! An architect is chosen, plans are drawn and a budget is set. As an elaborate model of the new structure is being built to display in the foyer, a committee is meeting and drawing up plans for the financial pledge campaign that is carefully designed to keep pace with every phase of the project. A master chart will detail what every volunteer worker is supposed to do and when. For several months, you will hear sermons and financial reports, receive newsletters and special mailings, and see pictures and graphs, all aimed at one thing—enlisting your participation in reaching the goal. Sometimes these efforts are so effective they go "over the top."

> *Within every church there are persons who, if asked, will become praying saints for your pastor.*

When starting to build a prayer hedge around your pastor, you need to have a similar mentality. It is a "building program" of another kind, one that will require every bit as much planning, organization and effort if it is to be done right. You will need leaders, goals, recruiting strategies, a budget, time, and preferably even a blueprint or model to follow. It always helps to know what the thing will look like after it is completed. Properly organized, building a prayer hedge can be fun—and a very rewarding experience for each person involved.

2. Share Your Intentions With Your Pastor

Let your pastor know this is a genuine move to bless and protect, and not some devious plot to expose or oust him. Ask for his advice and prayer concerns, and work in close concert with his desires. Be sensitive to the fact that there may have been, up until now, little interest in praying for him, so your sudden concern may actually seem a little alarming, or like an invasion of privacy. If this is the case, don't try to force the issue along too quickly. Be patient.

If either your pastor or your pastor's spouse seems skeptical, share a copy of this book with them. If you know of a church in your area that is effectively praying for their shepherd, let them know about that also. Take time to make sure they understand what you have in mind—be as transparent and open as possible. If your motivation is pure, their fears should dissipate as they gain understanding.

3. Identify Places Where a Hedge Might Grow

One of the easiest ways to build a prayer hedge for your pastor is to ask persons who are already praying in a systematic way to start praying specifically for their pastor. In other words, interface pastoral prayer with other ministries that are already in existence. Often the structure for a powerful prayer force is already in place in the form of Sunday school classes, Bible studies, women's groups or other organized prayer meetings. Don't overlook the wealth of resources available in your children's building and youth programs. Young people tend to be excellent pastor prayer partners because the responsibility makes them feel important, and they have no desire or reason to evaluate or criticize the pastor's performance. Their relative innocence gives them a different perspective than adult intercessors have, and sometimes a greater capacity for grace and faith.

If you already have a prayer room in your church, this is another excellent place to plant the seeds of a dynamic prayer hedge. With little expense, you can create a special place in it to remind those that are already coming to pray specifically for their pastor.

Years ago, when a man named Larry Lea pastored Church on the Rock in Rockwall, Texas, he developed a wonderful prayer station in their prayer room for his staff and their families. Beside their pictures were the following suggestions:

a. Pray that the pastors' private lives will be as strong as their public lives.

b. Pray that nothing will violate the anointing from without or from within.

c. Pray that the Lord will send in a great harvest of souls from the north, south, east and west.

d. Pray that the pastors will be delivered from unreasonably negative people.

e. Pray for the Lord to bless the church financially so the pastors can focus on ministry.

f. Pray that the Lord will place a hedge of protection around each of the pastors and their families.

Prayer rooms offer a marvelous way to soak a church and its leadership in prayer. Incidentally, you will notice that as you pray for your leaders, an atmosphere of affirmation and support will become more and more evident throughout all areas of your church. Honor is contagious.

1. WRITE DOWN A FEW NAMES OF PEOPLE WHO MIGHT TAKE A LEADERSHIP ROLE IN THE PRAYER HEDGE "BUILDING PROGRAM."

2. BRAINSTORM ABOUT PRAYER OPPORTUNITIES FOR YOUR PASTOR BEFORE AND DURING THE SUNDAY SERVICES.

3. WRITE DOWN AS MANY EXIST-
ING MINISTRIES AS YOU CAN THINK
OF WHERE PRAYER FOR THE PASTOR
COULD BE EASILY INCORPORATED.

Once you have explored all the possible places to plant prayer hedges in existing ministries, start thinking creatively about new ways in which you can enlist people to pray. For example, many pastors have a team of people that pray for them while they preach. Some meet with a prayer team prior to the Sunday morning services to share their concerns for that day and receive prayer directly. Others have prayer partners that pray throughout the week on specific days.

Other ideas might include regular Pastor Appreciation Sundays, unique prayer guides distributed in the bulletins, or special prayer vigils aimed at the pastor during times of crisis or difficulty. The appendix in the back of this book may help you brainstorm.

4. Determine How You Will Train Your Hedge

You are likely to find many people in your church who want to pray for their pastor, but don't know how. They will need to be trained. This study, and particularly the prayer helps in the next chapter, "The Power and Practice of Prayer," should be required reading.

Adapt the content as necessary to train young children.

Prayer Point Press also offers hundreds of other books on various aspects of prayer such as personal devotions and intercession that can help elevate the overall prayer literacy and aptitude of your congregation. I have heard it said that you can't mobilize what isn't there. If the personal prayer lives of the people in your church are weak to begin with, your job of mobilizing prayer for the pastor will be much more difficult. You may have to address the more general need in order to accomplish the specific goal.

However, don't make it harder than it has to be; just be realistic about your expectations. No one's prayers should be discounted or "graded;" certainly God does not relate to us in that way. But on the other hand, don't expect people to do mighty spiritual warfare on behalf of the pastor if they have never been introduced to the basic weapons of prayer. Start people praying at a level that they are comfortable with, gently challenging them over time with new materials and resources.

> *Start people praying at a level that they are comfortable with, gently challenging them over time with new materials and resources.*

One issue that merits mentioning here is that of confidentiality. As you will recall from the first chapter, fear is a big issue for many pastors when it comes to asking for and receiving prayer. This means that earning and keeping your pastor's trust is of paramount importance. One "slip" is all it takes to destroy a pastor's confidence in his hedge—it is the kind of mistake that can take years to repair. You must be discerning and wise when it comes to handling personal or sensitive requests, and you must emphasize with all those who pray that any information they receive is to be treated as confidential.

5. *Recruit Pray-ers*

a. Start small.

Start small and go for consistency and quality. As you branch out, quietly and routinely recruit people from different age-level groups in the church. Keep in mind that your hedge will grow larger and stronger over time—do not expect to enlist hundreds at a time.

Cindy Jacobs gives helpful advice to pastors who desire to build their own hedge, based on Jesus' words in Matthew 7:7, "Ask and it will be given to you; seek and you will find; knock and the door will be opened to you." She suggests two steps: (1) Ask. The first step is to pray and ask the Lord to set aside personal prayer partners on your behalf. (2) Seek. Make a list of those whom you feel might pray for you on a regular basis. She says to pastors:

> Listen to what people tell you as they go out the door
> of your church or after you speak. Some will say repeat-
> edly, 'I pray for you and your family every day.' Take
> time to interview these as to what they hear from God
> as they pray for you. If you are in the ministry, God has
> already set aside some who are to pray for you. Mobiliz-
> ing them for effectual intercession is usually a simple
> matter of recognizing what God has already done (163).

b. Look for maturity.

Throughout the past decade, James Dobson has been one of America's most renowned pastors, reaching millions every week with his television programs, video tapes, audio cassettes, books and seminars. The demands on his time would drive most pastors to distraction, but Dr. Dobson has been unwavering in his commitment to building Christian families.

His secret? For years he has had a one-man prayer force in long-time friend Nobel Hathaway. From his home in Boone, North Carolina,

Nobel has faithfully prayed for James and his family every day. This was his pledge of support: "I have committed my remaining days to continue the ministry that Dr. Dobson's parents started," Hathaway explained. "Every morning before breakfast, I have a 'one-man prayer meeting' for Jim, Shirley, Danae and Ryan. I bombard the skies with prayers for the Dobsons" (*Shield* 182-183).

Start your prayer hedge by choosing some of the most mature members of your church who are already praying. These proven and committed prayer warriors can be extremely faithful and powerful intercessors.

c. Recruit a wide range of partners.

A few years ago, Mark Rutland was conducting a seminar for pastors that caused him to be on his feet during most of the meeting. The pain had become so great from a nagging bone problem in his right foot that he was unable to stand and continue. So Mark asked those pastors with the gift of healing to come forward and pray for him. However, the pain continued.

As Dr. Rutland lay on one of the pews at the front of the church during a break contemplating how he could go on, a young boy with Down's syndrome walked down the center aisle. As he approached Dr. Rutland, he pulled out a toy gun, pointed it at the afflicted foot and said, "Bang, bang, Mark. Be healed in Jesus' name." Immediately the pain disappeared.

> *...he pulled out a toy gun, pointed it at the afflicted foot and said, "Bang, bang, Mark. Be healed in Jesus' name."*

I had a similar experience while conducting a prayer seminar years ago in Oklahoma City. The flu had gotten me down and, despite prayers being offered in my behalf, my condition was steadily growing worse. My fever was escalating, and I was growing weaker and weaker.

After I preached, I came down to the altar to visit with fellow worshipers. A woman who was confined to a wheelchair rolled toward me and I reached forward to clasp her hand. Because of a speech impediment, she had great difficulty speaking. I strained to understand her words. The dear soul was praying for me. Instantly, I was healed!

I love stories like these because they illustrate in such a powerful way the sovereignty of God and his total disregard for earthly achievements or stature. He often uses "the least of these" to accomplish mighty deeds in his name, especially through prayer. Keep in mind that our prayers are answered based on who Jesus is, not who we are, so there really are no qualifications except a pure heart. You may be surprised where you will find dedicated intercessors.

6. Anticipate Some Apathy

A laywoman in Michigan made the appeal for prayer in her church of 200, and only two people responded. It is not easy to plant a hedge because there is apathy in the soil. Where there is no root, the prayer hedge simply cannot grow. However, don't take resistance as the final answer. Rely on the Holy Spirit and go forward with your efforts in the name of Jesus.

8. Name Your Group

Although it seems like a trivial detail, you will probably want to name the group that prays for the pastor regularly. The group of men who prayed for me on Sunday mornings was called the "Gibborium," the Hebrew word meaning "mighty men." The Gibborium referred to King David's elite soldiers who went with him to guard him. Other names I have heard include The Watchmen, The Elijah Force and simply Prayer Partners. Naming a prayer hedge gives the members a sense of mission and camaraderie.

9. Set Specific Times to Pray

Give people you recruit a time frame in which to pray. Most of us today live by schedules, and we need to schedule prayer into our lives. For example, ask someone to pray for the pastor for six weeks, or maybe for three months. This is what I call "term praying," meaning that you announce when the term of praying begins and when it ends. Doing so will help your partners have a sense of fulfillment and closure to their commitment.

Prayer partners not only need a specific term to pray, they also need to know how often and how long they are to pray. For example, a pastor in Denver asks two or three different laypersons each Sunday morning to pray with her in her study for about 15 minutes. It's her unique way of introducing them to the idea of becoming part of regular prayer efforts in her behalf. Another pastor of a large church in Washington, D.C. enlisted 30 men to pray for him and then assigned each one a particular date of the month. Every Monday, he has breakfast with the seven for that week—and tells them what is before him so they can pray effectively. I know

4. WHAT IS "TERM PRAYING" AND WHY IS IT IMPORTANT?

5. HOW WILL PRAYING FOR YOUR PASTOR INFLUENCE THE OVERALL ATTITUDE TOWARD LEADERSHIP AND AUTHORITY IN YOUR CHURCH?

several pastors who have prayer partners who are on call to pray as needed for special events. While they do not intercede on a regular basis, these reinforcements are called on when the pastor has a tough funeral to conduct, a revival to preach, or an important meeting to attend. Some pastors have one or two very close intercessors that pray for them every day.

Regardless of what kind of schedule you set up, be sure to include prayer for the pastor as often as you can and in as many ways as you can during the worship services. Such modeling before the church sets a good example that others will see and follow.

10. Listen to the Holy Spirit

One afternoon, as I was driving my little Volkswagen home from seminary, I accidentally turned the wrong way down a one-way street. All I was thinking about was getting home. Maybe that's why I was oblivious to the traffic signals that were only visible in my rear view mirror. I had the road all to myself.

A split second later, I saw a huge truck pulling out straight into the side if my tiny car. The driver hit his brakes and screeched to a halt as I frantically swerved to avoid being squashed like a bug. In that moment, I experienced the true meaning of "divine intervention."

The next morning, one of my intercessors called to say that she had received a burden to ask Jesus to protect me the previous day. "What was going on yesterday around four o'clock?" she inquired. As I explained to her my close call, we both realized it was because of her prayers and the grace of God that I was not wiped out.

That incident happened over a quarter of a century ago, but it remains a vivid memory. I am reminded of it every time I get going the "wrong way" in life and am spared through the prayers of someone who is tuned in to the Holy Spirit.

Not all prayers can be scheduled. Encourage your partners to be sensitive to the presence of the Holy Spirit in their lives so they can immediately pray for your pastor's special needs.

11. Pray for Other Pastors

God did not place your pastor in your church just for the sake of your members. He also has a role for your shepherd to play in pastoring your entire city. In God's eyes, the body of Christ in your community is one, whether the churches there are walking out that reality or not. It honors him when you pray not only for your own pastor, but for the other pastors in the body of Christ.

> *Not all prayers can be scheduled.*

You can choose a different pastor in your city each week to pray for, or you can assign every pastor to a different prayer partner and ask them to pray for that person for a specified term. You might even encourage the intercessors to send prayer grams occasionally or to write out a prayer and mail it. What a beautiful, sincere way to help promote unity! You might be surprised at how well the other pastors will respond, knowing that someone is praying for them, expecting nothing in return.

"How good and pleasant it is when brothers live together in unity! ...For there the Lord bestows his blessing, even life forevermore" (Psalm 133:1, 3).

12. Act Now

Don't get so bogged down early on in developing elaborate plans that you fail to start. After you have touched base with your pastor to outline what you want to do, ask two or three members of your church to become founding members of your prayer group. Right away, ask them to start praying daily for your pastor and the success of the new prayer min-

6. WHY IS IT IMPORTANT TO KEEP
EPHESIANS 6:12 IN MIND AS YOU
INTERCEDE?

7. WHY PRAY FOR OTHER PASTORS
IN THE CITY?

istry. Ask your pastor to announce what you are doing from the pulpit and invite persons who are interested to contact you. In addition, put information about the pastoral prayer covering in your church newsletter and the Sunday worship bulletin. Just don't wait until you have everything figured out and in order.

Not long ago, I visited a former pastor in a Houston hospital. He confessed that he was hooked on cocaine. At one time, he was one of the best Bible teachers I knew, but he had lost everything. I asked him what happened, and he said, "I lost my prayer covering, and I was unable to stand alone." How tragic! With a well-planted prayer hedge, the story would probably have had a totally different outcome.

Remember, we are at war. The enemy comes to steal, kill and destroy. "For our struggle is not against flesh and blood, but against the rulers, against the authorities, against the powers of this dark world and against the spiritual forces of evil in the heavenly realms" (Ephesians 6:12).

The devil prowls around like a roaring lion looking for a pastor to devour, and his darts are literal. He fires at the flammable areas of their lives. He shoots criticism, immoral thoughts, fear of failure, unwholesome comparisons and self-doubts. He shot at the apostles in the book of Acts, and he will shoot at your leader. He tries to use power and prestige to bend a pastor toward the world. He often sets traps in counseling sessions to ensnare pastors into unhealthy relationships. He shoots barrages of flaming arrows at the pastor's spouse and children in an effort to destroy the parsonage family. He inflicts and infects with depression and attitudes of self-pity.

Satan's goal is for the pastor to be lonely, cut off and cast in a sea of despondence. Why? Revelation 12:12 answers: "He is filled with fury, because he knows that his time is short." Satan knows that the best way to cause confusion and division in the body of Christ is to render its leaders ineffective. If the pastor is listless and visionless, the sheep will be as well. Therefore, the enemy's assault is on the shepherd. No pastor is exempt. Pastors of large churches or small churches, holy men and holy women are all vulnerable to his attacks. Honest pastors are tempted to become otherwise.

The pressure never ceases, and it won't until we enter the kingdom of heaven. We are in enemy territory, and we need to cover our leaders in prayer to stand and even stand some more. The more effective a pastor is, the more he will be attacked.

CARING FOR THE HEDGE

As your prayer hedge begins to take shape, water and nurture it so that it will grow strong and healthy. It will be a dynamic, living thing that changes as it matures.

Definitely the most important ingredient in caring for the hedge is the affirmation of the pastor. If she encourages her prayer partners and gives them plenty of information and appreciation, they will remain committed and strong. However, if your pastor will not or can not take an active role in affirming the hedge, there are several things you can do to help meet that need.

1. Encourage the Prayer Hedge from the Pulpit

As much as possible, make prayer for the pastor an integral part of church life by reporting on it, validating it and modeling it as often as you can during worship services. It does not need to take up much time, but you need to keep it consistently visible to the congregation so that in time, people will understand it as foundational.

Your ultimate goal is not just to have a list of names who will pray. That is where you must start and it is important, but it is not the end. By praying for your shepherd, you want to create a stronghold—a system of entrenched attitudes, behaviors, and expectations—that honors the office of pastor as spiritual leader. The principle is this—where God sees honor bestowed upon his chosen representative, he will pour out his favor. As you honor your pastor by praying for him, you are creating a spiritual atmosphere that God can bless.

> *As you honor your pastor by praying for him, you are creating a spiritual atmosphere that God can bless.*

Note to Pastors: Your lay leaders can and should carry much of the burden of "advertising" the prayer hedge. Be wise enough to give them your blessing to do so. Do not dismiss it as unimportant or let false humility get in your way. But know this: There is no substitute for these words, "Please pray for me. I need your covering." Your people need to hear from your own mouth that prayer support is important to you.

2. Build Relationships Among the Hedge

Meet regularly with the prayer hedge, and particularly with the leaders and organizers. This gives you a chance to communicate requests, answers and other information, and also helps promote the team concept. Most intercessors do better when they feel a part of a group rather than feeling isolated.

Include the pastor as often as you can when the group gets together, but do not expect him to be there every time. Even a little bit of interaction with your shepherd will go a long way toward developing rapport and trust in the ministry.

Note to Pastors: This can be a turn-off to some of you, who already feel pulled to spend time with this group and that group. But your prayer partners don't need a lot of your time, they just need to know that you are interested enough to meet with them occasionally. If you have any close, personal intercessors, you might have lunch with them once a week. For general intercessors, once every month or so is probably enough. Their prayer times will mean more if they occasionally get to hear directly from you about your needs and how their prayers make a difference.

3. Foster Respect for Your Pastor's Time

To balance the last point, make sure that prayer partners understand that their role is to pray for the pastor, not spend time with him building a personal relationship. While some interaction will be inevitable and healthy, it is imperative that the hedge do more to protect the pastor's time than to impose upon it.

Make sure that meeting times with the pastor to communicate requests and feedback are agreed upon in advance and honored. Be very discretionary about "dropping by" the office to see how he's doing or calling just to chit-chat. Be friendly and sincere, but be wise and humble.

Another way to foster this attitude of respect is to encourage your pastor's time off, and do what you can to appropriate times of solitude for the pastoral couple. Ask the ruling board to give your pastor seasons or times to go away to a place of privacy and pray. Such retreats will renew and bless your leader in a multitude of ways.

4. Supply Plenty of Information

I have learned over the years that in any kind of prayer ministry, information is like fuel. It is one thing to say, "Pray for Pastor Barker this week," and a completely different thing to say, "Pray for Pastor Barker this week. He has to conduct a funeral on Tuesday for a 12-year-old girl, he's having lunch with the mayor on Thursday, and his son has been sick with the flu."

While it is possible to pray for someone without knowing really anything about their situation, your prayers take on a whole new passion when you understand the specific needs in that person's life. Information stirs creativity and gives pray-ers the ability to pinpoint the need with appropriate scriptures.

Note to Pastors: Be as specific as you can be about your requests with the various parts of your hedge. Be transparent with them to the degree of trust that you assign to the different levels in your own intercessory circles. Share your visions, goals, preaching texts, study times and stressful times of counseling or ministry. Look for ways to encourage them to pray God's word over you. You may even want to write a prayer guide specifically for them.

5. Give Lots of Feedback

When possible, give the hedge feedback about answered prayers, and get feedback from them concerning what they are hearing as they pray. Doing so will make them feel genuinely good about what they are doing and will give them an incentive to continue praying. Keep communication flowing between the pray-ers and your pastor, whether it is through notes, phone messages or email. If information is like fuel, then positive feedback is like dynamite. Proclaiming answers to prayer in your pastor's behalf can cause your pastoral prayer ministry to explode!

Listen to how the apostle Paul encouraged his prayer hedge, "Then many will give thanks on your behalf for the gracious favor granted us in answer to the prayers of many" (2 Corinthians 1:11).

Note to Pastors: Share with your hedge specific things God does in answer to their prayers. The time and effort you spend to communicate positive feedback and results will come back to you one hundred fold.

6. Pray for Them

Ask the Lord to send intercessors who will pray for your pastor, and be faithful to thank him when he does.

Note to Pastors: If you are fortunate enough to have a hedge raised up

8. How could prayer team leaders deal with a team member who "pesters" the pastor with frequent phone calls, etc.?

9. What are some other "sticky" situations that might arise? How would they be dealt with?

around you and your family, let me encourage you to pray for those who pray for you. Do not expect to match their time commitment—that is not the objective. But set aside some time each week to lift them up by name to God.

It is impossible to measure the value of one who stands in the gap for your preaching, intercedes on behalf of your spouse and children, and cries out to God for you in the wee hours of the night. But some of your prayer partners will do exactly that, and it is a good practice for you to pray God's blessing upon them in return. You may want to keep their pictures or names in your Bible as a visible reminder of your covering.

7. Appreciate Them

Although you can never really expect to repay them, find creative ways to appreciate all the pastoral prayer partners at least once or twice a year. Have a banquet or party. Attend a special event as a group. Perhaps you could even plan a retreat. When I pastored, my wife and I invited all of our intercessors over for burnt offerings (hamburgers and hot dogs) about every six months, and it was always one of my favorite church functions.

Note to Pastors: Consider thanking your partners from the pulpit, in the bulletin, or in the church newsletter to honor their commitment before the congregation. Also, depending on how many you have, you might develop a system of periodically calling them personally to thank them. This will help you retain your most active members, reactivate partners who have become inactive, and recruit new partners.

IN YOUR PASTOR'S HONOR

Do you realize that the Catholic Church has existed for more than one thousand years, in nearly every nation of the world, without splitting?

It's amazing, given the relatively short and rocky history of some other major religious institutions.

I have to wonder if the longevity of Catholicism is not, at least in part, a result of "honoring" prayer. For example, in every mass ever conducted, prayers are offered for the Pope and the bishop of the diocese by name. Imagine how many prayers are lifted up for the Pope in a single week! It might just be that, because this church prays for its leaders, Satan has found no foothold to divide it.

Numbers 16 tells an interesting story. Korah, Dathan and Abiram were not happy with the conditions in their community, so they went as a group to confront Moses and Aaron, their shepherds. They questioned Moses as their appointed leader, and they asked Moses and Aaron, "Why, then do you set yourselves above the Lord's assembly?" Perhaps Korah, Dathan and Abiram felt that they were equally qualified to lead the Israelites to the promised land.

When Moses heard their opposition, he proposed a "trial by fire," telling them, "In the morning, the Lord will show who belongs to him and who is holy." When the assembly gathered early the next day, God opened up the earth and swallowed Korah, Dathan and Abiram and all of their possessions and households—hymnals and all. I would guess that scene pretty much secured Moses's position of leadership in the Israeli camp.

> *...God takes it personally when we fail to honor him through our shepherds.*

The office of pastor is representative of God in the local church, and God takes it personally when we fail to honor him through our shepherds. It is not that they are perfect or any less sinful than we are. But somehow in the economy of God, the way we treat our pastors reveals the attitude of our hearts toward God.

10. IN LIGHT OF THE STORY IN
NUMBERS 16, DISCUSS THE STATE-
MENT, "WHEN A CHURCH FAILS TO
HONOR THE OFFICE OF
PASTOR...THE CHURCH DISHONORS
GOD."

11. WHAT EVIDENCE DO YOU SEE
OF THIS SPIRITUAL PRINCIPLE
WORKING TODAY?

When a church fails to honor the office of pastor—no matter who the person is—the church dishonors God. To accuse and belittle a pastor without praying for him offends God, and when God is offended, the ground opens up to swallow the church's blessings, effectiveness and authority in the community. In other words, if we cannot honor the pastor whom we can see, how can we honor God whom we cannot see?

I believe a prayer hedge around the pastor honors her, because the highest honor you can give someone is to pray for her. And where honor is given, God will bestow victory and blessing. In other words, taking your pastor for granted is a sin! The reason a few dissenters can harm a pastor is because the 95 percent of the congregation who like and support her are not mobilized to pray for her. When you build a hedge of prayer around your pastor, you honor your pastor and you honor God.

Jonathan Edwards (1703-1758), the famous early American preacher, once said:

> If some Christians
> that had been com-

plaining about their minister had said and acted less before men and had applied themselves with all their might
to cry to God for their ministers—had, as it were, risen
and stormed heaven with their humble, fervent, and in-
cessant prayers for them—they would have been much
more in the way of success (Neighbour 19).

Don't go to the phone; go to the throne! A pastor not prayed for is
preyed upon. The more a pastor threatens the enemy, the more severe
will be the attacks.

Jesus set the example for us when he prayed for his shepherds-in-
training, the disciples, saying:

"Holy Father, protect them by the power of your
name—the name you gave me.... My prayer is not that
you take them out of the world but that you protect
them from the evil one" (John 17:11-15).

God desires for your pastor to be fruitful (John 15:8)—he is called
to be fulfilled and happy in his work. He deserves wisdom, anointing,
rest, opportunities to share Christ, rich sermons, financial freedom, good
family time, a keen sense of fulfillment, realistic time management, vision
and creativity. Through prayer, you can lay claim to this inheritance in his
behalf. You are the key to lifting your pastor's battle-weary hands as
Aaron and Hur lifted Moses' hands, keeping your pastor protected through
all areas of ministry.

CHAPTER SIX

THE POWER AND PRACTICE _
of Prayer

One day, while my wife was at home washing dishes she suddenly stopped. She sensed something. Perhaps it was a slight variation in temperature, or an unexplainable quietness that—in a second or two—encompassed the space around her. Standing there with soap bubbles on her hands, her pulse quickened as she felt an urgent need to pray for our oldest son, Travis. "His life is in danger," she thought.

She slipped off her apron, bowed her head, and opened her heart to God in prayer. From Psalm 91 and Luke 10:19, she knew God's promise of protection, and she prayed in Jesus' name in the Holy Spirit.

Travis was definitely in danger. As she prayed, our son was racing out of town at 120 miles per hour on a motorcycle that was, at best, unsafe. When he finally brought the bike to a stop, the back tire went completely flat. Without my wife's immediate response to the nudging of the Spirit, he would have been dead.

One whisper. One prayer. One life saved.

"Amazing," you say? Not really. "Impossible?" Oh no. Remember the story mentioned earlier about Moses, Aaron and Hur (Exodus 17)? Two armies, clad in armor, trained in battle, and led by generals faced off with each other. Swords clashed, chariots raced, men shouted and fell dead in the fury of hand-to-hand combat. Yet the victory was determined not by war strategies, but by the three men on the mountain. As Moses prayed, and as Aaron and Hur lifted his hands, Joshua and the Israelites prevailed.

What a testimony to the power of prayer!

COVENANT PRAYER

The power of prayer is rooted in the biblical concept of covenant. In planting a prayer hedge, it is important to understand this covenant theology, and why it is the basis for all prayer.

In Exodus 34:10, the Lord said to Moses:

> I am making a covenant with you. Before all your people
> I will do wonders never before done in any nation in all
> the world. The people you live among will see how
> awesome is the work that I, the Lord, will do for you.

The central idea in a covenant is commitment. God was promising in Exodus to commit himself to man in a redemptive process that man would reciprocate in a commitment to God.

The Hebrew word for covenant means "to cut until blood flows." This form of covenant was the most serious kind in the Old Testament. When men entered a blood covenant, it was for life. They exchanged coats as a symbol of their identities being merged. They gave weapons to vow protection for each other. They also exchanged names to give the other access to their own property and rights. Finally, they would cut their wrists, press them together, and let the life blood flow between them to symbolize the binding nature of the covenant. If the covenant was broken, death could be the penalty. Divorce was out of the question. Old Testament covenant was extremely serious.

> *A prayer hedge needs to be seen in the light and depth of covenant.*

Beginning with Noah, God would initiate a series of covenants with Abraham, Moses and David to reveal his love for us in a commitment that would culminate in the new covenant ratified by his Son. The old covenant was but a shadow of a better one to come. In the old covenant, the principles of prayer are set in motion to be later fulfilled in the person of Jesus Christ.

A prayer hedge needs to be seen in the light and depth of covenant. Prayer is powerful not so much because of our commitment to God, but because of the Lord's commitment to us. Covenant prayer is the vehicle for his interaction and provision in our lives. Through the new covenant, God invests himself in us to make us his people.

Let me explain. Covenant prayer teaches us that the purpose of prayer is not just to "get something" from God—it is a means of knowing God personally and intimately.

God wants us to be his people. He tells us:

> I will take you as my own people, and I will be your God. Then you will know that I am the Lord your God.... Now if you obey me fully and keep my covenant, then out of all nations you will be my treasured possession. Although the whole earth is mine, you will be for me a kingdom of priests and a holy nation" (Exodus 6:7, 19:5).

Jesus said it like this:

> As the Father has loved me, so have I loved you. Now remain in my love. If you obey my commandments, you will remain in my love, just as I have obeyed my Fathers's commands and remain in his love. I have told you this so that my joy may be in you complete.... I have called you friends, for everything that I learned from my Father I have made known to you (John 15:9-11, 15).

Prayer is the act of being bound in love to our God. Further, the Father seeks to display his glory and majesty in us. He wants to see us redeemed and victorious over our enemies. He desires to guide us and see his kingdom displayed in us, his people. As his splendor is displayed in us, his glory is manifest and the world will see and believe (John 2:11). In the idea of covenant, all that is his is ours, and all that is ours is his.

Prayer is the mysterious means by which we interact with our heavenly Father. It is the covenant vehicle for the people of God to receive his glory.

In both the old and new covenants, we see this dynamic. For example, Deuteronomy 4:29 says, "But if from there you seek the Lord your God, you will find him if you look for him with all your heart and with all your soul." This is the Old Testament basis for "calling" upon God in personal and corporate prayer.

In the New Testament, Jesus said:

> Ask and it will be given you; seek and you will find; knock and the door will be opened to you. For everyone who asks receives; he who seeks finds; and to him who knocks, the door will be opened. ...[H]ow much more will your Father in heaven give good gifts to those who ask him! (Matthew 7:7-8; 11).

Prayer enables us to know God and to ever receive his manifold provision like Aaron, Moses and Hur did. As those three men on the mountain prayed, the Amalekites found out they were not just fighting against the Israelites, but against the Lord God almighty!

As we pray to access the new covenant, we are praying in agreement with God's will. Jesus tells us in Matthew that if two or three on earth agree in prayer about anything, it will be done by the Father in heaven, because when we agree in prayer with other believers, he is in our midst. Agreement is covenant language, and it is powerful.

If you don't understand something your pastor says or does, instead of criticizing him, just pray in agreement with God's highest and best, and trust the two of them to work out the details together. When you pray for a shepherd, regardless of the circumstances, you are in agreement with the Father's will and desire.

Prayer hedges make sense when you understand covenant commitment and relationship. The whole concept

1. IN OUR COVENANT RELATIONSHIP, "ALL THAT IS GOD'S IS OURS AND ALL THAT IS OURS IS GOD'S." LIST THINGS THAT GOD BRINGS TO THE RELATIONSHIP:

LIST WHAT WE BRING TO THE RELATIONSHIP:

of covenant makes available to you the resources of God on behalf of your shepherd to equip him for the calling of ministry.

ACCESS TO THE COVENANT

A man I consider to be one of my closest friends in the ministry is Gregg Parris, pastor of Union Chapel United Methodist Church in Muncie, Indiana. In December, 1989 Gregg's wife, Beth, was diagnosed with cancer. The prognosis was not good.

Over a period of six months, Beth went through surgery, radiation and chemotherapy. There were some very dark days for the couple—times when the outcome could easily have gone one way or the other.

"It was a very stressful time in our lives," Gregg shares. "I have known the blessing of being an intercessor for many people with life-threatening problems, but this was the first time I encountered the profound and unmistakable benefits of the prayer covenant that Beth and I have with God."

For Gregg, nothing could have been more real. "It was the most amazing experience," he says. "Beth and I were buoyed up, sustained and protected by the grace of God that came to us through the intercessory prayers of our lay people."

Today, Gregg still testifies that words cannot describe the peace of the Lord that he and his wife came to know. "Through the loving, fervent and sincere prayers of God's people, my wife and I discovered that the Lord can cause light to shine in the darkest of places."

In the Bible, the name of God is the key to accessing the covenant in God's will and character. For example, Deuteronomy 12:5 states, "but you are to seek the place the Lord your God will choose from among all your tribes to put his Name there for his dwelling. To that place you must go..." His name in covenant represents his presence, his character, his holiness and his greatness. To take his name in vain is to miss this understanding.

In the Old Testament, seven covenant names were given to the people to access the covenant provisions in prayer. They are:

Jehovah—The Great I Am (Exodus 3:14)

Jehovah Jireh—The Provider (Exodus 22:14)

El Shaddai—The Lord God Almighty (Genesis 49:24-25)

Adonai—Our Shield (Genesis 15:1-3)

Jehovah Rophi—The Healer (Exodus 15:26)

Jehovah M Kadesh—The Righteous One (Leviticus 20:7-8)

Jehovah Nissi—Our Banner (Exodus 17:15)

To know God's name in covenant was to know him personally, and the blessing of the covenant was made available. As people called upon his name, they were blessed in right-standing, holiness, mercy and healing. The aspect of blessing was particularly strong in the Abrahamic covenant.

Today, when we pray in the name of Jesus, we are still blessed through God's covenant with Abraham. Through his blood, Christ transformed the old covenant into a new one, making all the same provisions available to us through *one* name. Since the old covenant was secured through the blood of Jesus, it is through his name alone that we access the new covenant.

Therefore, you can bless your pastor through prayer in Jesus' name. He said, "And I will do whatever you ask in my name, so that the son may bring glory to the Father. You may ask me for anything in my name, and I will do it" (John 14:13-14). Several times Jesus told us to pray in his name, and remembering the old covenant, his name represents his personhood, character and power.

In addition to accessing the covenant, praying in Jesus' name also protects us from praying human-centered prayers. Covenant prayer is not me getting my will done in heaven. It is agreeing with God and getting his will done on earth. Prayer in Jesus' name is not for improving my golf game or getting a parking space at the mall, it is praying in line with his desires and his holiness. For example, to pray in Jesus' name is to pray for healing, peace and salvation for the lost. It is to pray for the strength to overcome temptation and resist the devil, and for the will to forgive and to reconcile. These are requests in line with the "anything" Jesus spoke of in John 14. God warns us against human-centered prayer, saying:

> *[Covenant prayer] is agreeing with God and getting his will done on earth.*

> You do not have, because you do not ask God. When you ask, you do not receive, because you ask with wrong motives, that you may spend what you get on your pleasures (James 4:2-3).

Covenant praying in Jesus' name is like the power of attorney—it means we have the power to act on earth in accordance with our God in heaven with whom we are "bonded." Jesus died on the cross, and was raised from the dead to take his seat in the heavenlies. He was the man who kept covenant with God so that we could pray and minister in his stead on the earth.

A prayer hedge in Jesus' name fully represents his will and interests in kingdom matters. For example, the enemy has a quiver full of darts of fear that he will use against a pastor—the fear of people and their opinions, the fear of opposition, the fear of taking a stand against abortion or racial injustice. However, we know that fear is not of God. So, in Jesus' name, in accordance with his will, prayer warriors can bind and stand against fear aimed at a pastor. The personhood of Jesus and the finished work of

Calvary stand as an ensign and force against the enemy's attempt to undermine a pastor's confidence with fear.

Praying in Jesus' name also protects and emboldens a pastor for Jesus. In Acts 4, Peter and John had been threatened not to preach in the name of Jesus. When the members of their prayer hedge met, they prayed:

> Now, Lord, consider their threats and enable your servants to speak your word with great boldness. Stretch out your hand to heal and perform miraculous signs and wonders through the name of your holy servant Jesus (Acts 4:29-30).

The answer was quick to come, "After they prayed, the place where they were meeting was shaken. And they were all filled with the Holy Spirit and spoke the word of God boldly" (Acts 4:31).

It is vital to understand that our prayers in behalf of the pastor are not just to be spoken in the name of Jesus, they are also heard in the name of Jesus. God hears us based on the finished work of Jesus on the cross, not based on our own holiness. Effective prayer is not just a matter of duty, technique or volume. It is a matter of Jesus and his righteousness applied to our petitions. A prayer hedge on behalf of a pastor is effective because God answers based on the covenant that was ratified by his Son. The force and power of a prayer hedge is in the name of Jesus.

> *God hears us based on the finished work of Jesus on the cross, not based on our own holiness.*

THE HOLY SPIRIT AND PRAYER HEDGES

One of the most powerful prayer hedges that ever met was in the upper room right after the ascension.

In the first chapter of Acts, Jesus gave his disciples some final instructions. He told them not to leave Jerusalem but to wait for the Father to pour out the Holy Spirit upon them so that they would be empowered to witness. Then Jesus was taken up before their eyes to be with the Father. So the disciples returned to Jerusalem and the upper room to wait as Jesus had told them, and "to pray continually."

What happened next changed the course of history, and is still relevant today. In Acts 2, the Holy Spirit was poured out in a powerful manner just as Jesus had promised, and the disciples amazed the Jews in Jerusalem with their preaching. Pastor Peter delivered one sermon and 3,000 souls were saved!

What the early church pastors needed and received in this holy unction, contemporary pastors desperately need today. When you pray for your pastor, you invite the Holy Spirit to come upon him with new anointing. As your pastor preaches and ministers to people, the Spirit will manifest the presence and power of God through him supernaturally.

Even Jesus prayed to receive this anointing of the Holy Spirit during his ministry here on earth. In Luke 3:21, we read, "When all the people were being baptized, Jesus was baptized too. And as he was praying, heaven was opened and the Holy Spirit descended on him in bodily form like a dove." Again in Luke 5:16, we read, "But Jesus often withdrew to lonely places and prayed," and the next verse states, "and the power of the Lord was present for him to heal the sick." Later, Luke 6:12 says, "One of those days Jesus went out into the hills to pray, and spent the whole night praying to God." Then verse 19 says that people were trying to touch him "because power was coming from him and healing them all."

The Holy Spirit came to Jesus when he prayed, and likewise he will come to us when we pray. Even the very Son of God knew the importance of praying to invite the Spirit's anointing. Jesus did not try to preach or heal without this power source. That is why, before the ascension, he instructed his first pastors to stay in Jerusalem until they had been "clothed with power from on high." He knew they needed that power to spread the gospel.

Jesus made it clear that the same power is available to us through prayer, "If you then, though you are evil, know how to give good gifts to your children, how much more will your Father in heaven give the Holy Spirit to those who ask him!" (Luke 11:13). Prayer is a means of grace and anointing to equip us for the work of God. This was clearly seen in the book of Acts.

If anything is clear in the old covenant, it is this—God wanted people unto himself who were his own treasured possession. These people who bore his name and nature would be holy. They were to be so distinct that the other nations would take notice (Exodus 34:10). It would be impossible to hide the fact that these people were "bonded" to an almighty and everlasting God. His love for them would be very evident. They would be blessed in every way and they would be healthy (Deuteronomy 7:6-8, 13-15). They

2. LIST SEVERAL REASONS WHY WE PRAY IN THE NAME OF JESUS:

3. WHY IS THE ANOINTING OF THE HOLY SPIRIT SO CRITICAL TO YOUR PASTOR'S SUCCESS IN MINISTRY? (REFER TO ACTS 1:8, JOHN. 6:44).

would know his glory and presence.

The outpouring of the Holy Spirit in Acts 2 amplified these intentions for the old covenant in the new covenant. The early church was the embodiment of all that the old covenant held to be true. But astonishingly, in the new covenant, the Holy Spirit would not just come upon a tent in the wilderness, or the holy place in the temple. He would fill every believer in Jesus! What an awesome thing!

This new creation, God's people, would fan out from the upper room to manifest his presence in worship and demonstrate his greatness with signs and wonders. Prayer hedges would be planted and the fruits of the Spirit would begin to happen.

Pastors are blessed by the Holy Spirit as people pray. When we

> *Pastors are blessed by the Holy Spirit as people pray.*

humble ourselves in prayer, we are emptied out, and like a wind, the Spirit rushes in and fills us with power for his work. The name and personhood of Jesus are exalted as a result of prayer hedges.

WHAT SHOULD YOU PRAY?

They seemed like the perfect couple. Ken was captain of his college football team; Linda was his favorite cheerleader. They were married a few weeks before Ken entered seminary. His professors called him "brilliant."

In 1985, Ken became the pastor of a fledgling church in one of the wealthiest coastal cities of southern California. Within a year, the membership had doubled and ground was being broken for a new sanctuary. During the same time, Linda became the marketing director of a small computer company. With her help, sales quadrupled.

Things kept moving upward until Ken hit 40. Feeling the effects of middle-age, he needed affirmation that he was still as handsome, still as "in demand" as he was in his 20's. Linda, five years Ken's junior, was just hitting her peak in the professional world. Except for regularly attending Sunday school and church, she had "a life of her own."

Circumstances could not have been better for Samantha, a 29-year-old bit part player in the movies who was anxious to establish her independence from her husband, a wealthy screen writer who had developed "other interests." When Samantha started coming to Ken for counseling, she turned on the charm. Flattered by the sorely needed affirmation, so did he. Soon they were playing tennis and having lunch together on a regular basis. As one member of the church observed, they "bonded."

When Ken began paying less attention to Linda, she devoted more time to traveling with the just-divorced president of her company. They became what the church secretary described as "inseparable."

As a courtesy to the once happily married couple, their church offered to pay for counseling. But it was too late. "The only counseling I need is from a divorce lawyer," Ken said. Linda, realizing the relationship was severely damaged, agreed. "We've become the gossip of the entire community," she said. "It's best to end it now, before the church has to suffer any more embarrassment."

Sadly, although many members saw what was happening to their pastor and his wife, no one did anything to intervene. The "situation" came up frequently in small groups and meetings, but everyone felt too awkward and uncomfortable to approach the subject with Ken or Linda. Speaking on behalf of the church, one of the lay leaders said, "We simply didn't know what to do!"

Pastors with problems need prayer, not gossip. Unfortunately, the members of Ken's church had overlooked prayer as a viable weapon to combat the forces of evil coming against him. They didn't know how.

They didn't know what to pray!

Intercessors need to know how to pray before there is an attack. You don't wait until the enemy is coming over the hill before you teach soldiers how to load and shoot their guns. Such training is given at boot camp—well ahead of the battle.

So, how should you pray?

Praying the Word

In Jeremiah 1:12, the Lord says, "You have seen correctly, for I am watching to see that my word is fulfilled." In Psalm 145:18, David declares, "The Lord is near to all who call on him, to all who call on him in truth." Jesus said it this way:

> If you remain in me and my words remain in you, ask whatever you wish, and it will be given you. This is to my Father's glory, that you bear much fruit, showing yourselves to be my disciples (John 15:7-8).

As God gives us access to the new covenant in Jesus' name, he provides the vocabulary of covenant prayer in his word. The covenant is based on God's faithful promises to his people, and our response to him is to keep his word in our hearts. Deuteronomy 28:2 and 13 state:

> All these blessings will come upon you and accompany you if you obey the Lord your God.... If you pay attention to the commands of the Lord your God that I give you this day and carefully follow them, you will always be at the top, never at the bottom.

The Lord told Joshua:

> Do not let this book of the Law depart from your mouth; meditate on it day and night, so that you may be careful to do everything written in it. Then you will be prosperous and successful (Joshua 1:8).

God's commitment to us is declared and recorded in his word. So as covenant people, we can expect him to uphold his promises just as they are written. Therefore, when you pray for your pastor, the prayers should be rooted in scripture. Pray what the Bible says for and about your pastor, because God's word offered back to him in prayer will not return void.

Reginald Klimionok calls praying the scriptures "truth praying." He writes, "Truth praying is a system of praying which encourages each Christian to pray out the great truths of God" (26).

The essence of truth praying is not to pray the problem or the need, but to lift to God what he has already promised in his word. This kind of praying builds faith.

The word is God's will for us, and we know that if we pray his will, he hears us and answers us (1 John 5:14-15). For example, the Bible teaches us that it is God's will for the lost to be saved. Proverbs 11:30 says "he who wins souls is wise." Thus, a prayer hedge could pray, "Lord, let my pastor be wise in soul

4. LIST SEVERAL ADVANTAGES OF SCRIPTURE PRAYING:

1.

2.

3.

4.

5.

5. FIND AT LEAST TWO SCRIPTURAL PROMISES THAT YOU COULD PRAY OVER YOURSELF AND YOUR FAMILY.

1.

2.

winning and focused on seeking and winning the lost. Give my pastor your burden so that none shall perish. This is your will. So be it." In the same manner, you could pray for your pastor to heal the sick, which is also God's will. Since God is a promise-keeping God, your pastor can see souls saved and the sick healed and Jesus will be glorified through it all.

> *A scriptural focus...brings the church into positive agreement concerning God's will and intent for the shepherd.*

In Ephesians 6, Paul lists the full armor of God as a source of protection and blessing. This is an excellent passage to pray over pastors to protect them as they do battle with the enemy! Remember, the forces of evil will use darts of skepticism, denial, disunity, seduction, coercion, disaster, depression and sickness against a pastor. The enemy is the antithesis of everything Jesus Christ stands for. Appendix B in the back of this book contains a prayer guide based on Ephesians 6 called "Hedging in the Pastor" that you can use to cover your pastor with the full armor of God.

Scripture praying is so rich in variety and creativity that prayer will not be repetitive, mundane or boring. You can find countless passages in addition to Ephesians 6 that can be prayed over your pastor, such as Psalm 23. Can you imagine the power of a number of people speaking this prayer for the pastor?

> The Lord is my pastor's shepherd; he or she will lack no good thing. You, Lord, give my pastor rest. Restore my pastor's energy. Guide my pastor in the paths of righteousness for your name's sake. Let no fear come near the parsonage. Comfort and anoint him or her, and let my pastor's cup overflow! And Lord, as a church we are in agreement that goodness and mercy will follow our pastor everywhere, and he or she will richly dwell in your

presence. Amen.

A scriptural focus like this brings the church into positive agreement concerning God's will and intent for the shepherd. How much better this is than gossip or "friendly fire!"

Covenant praying in the form of a prayer hedge is based on God's word. When we pray the scriptures, we humbly remind him what he has promised us, and in Jesus' name we receive these promises based on what he did on the cross. Peter summed it up in 2 Peter 1:3-4:

> His divine power has given us everything we need for life and godliness through our knowledge of him who called us by his own glory and goodness. Through these he has given us his very great and precious promises, so that through them you may participate in the divine nature and escape the corruption in the world caused by evil desires.

Prayers For My Pastor

Use the following prayers, in addition to the "Hedging in the Pastor" prayer guide in Appendix B, to pray for your shepherd (Teykl):

1. I thank you Father that your eyes are on my shepherd and your ears are attentive to my pastor's prayers and your face is against those who plot evil against my pastor (1 Peter 3:12). For I know that in all things you work for the good of _____ who loves you (Romans 8:28).

Will you not graciously give my pastor this city for Christ? And who can accuse this pastor who is daily interceded for by Jesus? (Romans 8:32-34). Therefore, in all things my pastor is more than a conqueror (Romans 8:37). Thank you, God.

2. Lord, we pray for discernment in exposing any schemes of the enemy against our pastor. Show us how to pray against all powers of this

dark world and the spiritual forces of darkness in heavenly realms. And, Lord, protect us as we wage warfare on behalf of our pastor (Ephesians 6:11-12). Amen.

> "Father, I thank you that no weapons formed against my pastor will prosper."

3. Father, I thank you that no weapons formed against my pastor will prosper. Every tongue raised against my shepherd will be cast down. Rumors and gossip will be turned aside. For _____ will be still before the Lord and wait on you. My pastor will dwell in the shadow of the most high God and will be delivered from terror, darts of doubt, and diseases (Psalm 91:5-6). Set your angels about my pastor (Psalm 91:11) and no power of the enemy shall harm _____ (Luke 10:19). Thank God forevermore!

4. Lord, let_____ have a discerning mind to prioritize the precious minutes in the day. Let my pastor discern what is most important and be guarded against the tyranny of the urgent (2 Corinthians 11:14; 1 John 4:1).

5. Father, allow my pastor to glory only in the cross (Galatians 6:14). Keep my pastor from pride and pity. Let the cross be his or her reason for ministry. Amen.

6. Renew my pastor in the Holy Spirit. Let my pastor wait and mount up with wings (Isaiah 40:27-31). Quicken my shepherd's body with the Holy Spirit (Romans 8:11). Renew _____'s vision and confidence (1 John 5:13-14). Revive my pastor's boldness to stand in strong personal conviction (Acts 4:29-31). Amen.

7. Jesus, keep my pastor holy in every way (1 Peter 1:16). Protect my shepherd from seducing spirits especially when he or she is tired and hard-pressed. Give _____ comrades to help protect him or her, and to share with in personal holiness (James 4:7). As my pastor draws near to

you, draw near to my pastor (James 4:8). Cancel the power of sin to have no effect (Ephesians 1:22). Amen.

8. I pray that the eyes of my pastor may be enlightened to know the hope to which we are called and know the riches of our glorious inheritance in the saints. Let my pastor know the incomparable great power which is in us who believe (Ephesians 1:18-19). Let _____ see the full revelation of Jesus Christ (Galatians 1:12) and place in this pastor a desire to know Christ and the power of his resurrection (Philippians 3:10). Amen.

9. Lord, deliver Pastor _____ from the tyranny of the unfinished. Grant my pastor a sense of fulfillment and the personal joy of Jesus (1 Timothy 6:6; John 15:11). Amen.

10. Lord, as our shepherd spends quiet time with you, shed your love abroad in his or her heart. Let my pastor know how much he or she is loved (Romans 5:5). In Jesus' name let the love of God be my pastor's mainstay in ministry. So be it!

11. Lord, I lift up the hands of my pastor and his or her family. Place them in the shelter of the Most High to rest in the shadow of the Almighty. I will say of the Lord, you are their refuge and fortress. You will preserve their family time. You will cover their home. Your faithfulness will meet their financial needs in Christ Jesus (Philippians 4:19). You will command your angels to guard them as they travel and win the lost. You have said, "I will be with them in trouble, I will deliver them and honor them and with a long life, I will satisfy them and show them my salvation" (Psalm 91). In Jesus' name I cancel all assignments of the enemy against them (Matthew 6:10). Amen.

12. In Jesus' name I speak to church hurts, abuse and ungrateful forces to move. I speak to mountains of criticism and inordinate expectations to be cast into the sea. I speak to stress, excessive phone counseling

and fatigue to be cast into the sea, and I believe every need, vision, and dream of _____ 's will be completed (Mark 11:22-24; Philippians 4:19). Amen.

13. Forgive those who hurt _____ and speak against him or her, and may he or she walk in forgiveness (Ephesians 4:32, 5:1). Guard my pastor from futile thinking (Ephesians 4:17) and a vain imagination. Let every thought be taken captive to obey Christ (2 Corinthians 10:3-5).

14. Lord Jesus, I know that in the course of pastoring, _____ is thrilled over conversions and changed lives. Yet I also realize that my pastor hears bad news and sad stories and ministers to those who are dying. Therefore, keep my shepherd ever before your face in worship (Matthew 4:10). Let my pastor see you and enjoy your presence ever more (Psalm 112:7). Let goodness and mercy follow my pastor all the days of his or her life (Psalm 23:6) and let my pastor's cup overflow (Psalm 23:5). Amen.

15. In Jesus' name we bind the fear of failure and the fear of humankind (John 14:1). Let _____ 's confidence not be eroded by the daily resistance to the gospel or his or her vision. Allow my pastor to fear God more than people. Amen.

16. Father, heal my shepherd's heart of any grief caused by ministry. Bestow on my pastor a crown of beauty instead of ashes and anoint him or her with the oil of gladness instead of mourning. Clothe my shepherd with a garment of praise instead of a spirit of depression. I call my pastor an oak of righteousness, a planting of the Lord to display your splendor (Isaiah 61:3). Amen.

17. Jesus, you said, "Do not let your hearts be troubled. Trust in God; trust also in me.... Peace I leave with you; my peace I give you" (John 14:1, 27). Apply these promises to _____. Let my pastor know the plans you have for him or her, plans to prosper, plans to give hope and a future (Jeremiah 29:11). Amen.

18. Keep my pastor in the midst of good and exciting worship. Keep my pastor from the traditions of men and religion which hold the form of godliness, but deny its power (2 Timothy 3:5). Give _____ a vision of heaven (Isaiah 6; Revelation 4). Amen.

19. With my shield of faith I cover my shepherd's mind to quench all flaming darts of doubt or vain imagination or mental distractions (Mark 6:5-6). Let the mind of Christ be strong in my pastor. Amen.

20. Lord, I stand against the enemies of my pastor's life—"busyness" (Acts 6:2-4), compulsions, compromise (Acts 5), unnecessary phone calls, chronic counselees, fatigue, sleepiness (Matthew 26:41), appetites, television, late meetings, over-commitments and doubt. Let nothing hinder _____'s time with you. Let my pastor rise up to seek you (Mark 1:35), pray with other pastors (Acts 1:14), and pray without ceasing (1 Thessalonians 5:17). Give my pastor the time, the desire and the place to pray (Acts 16:16). I rebuke in the name of Jesus any distractions from my pastor's devotional life (Mark 5:36). Amen.

> *Clothe my shepherd with a garment of praise instead of a spirit of depression.*

21. Send the spirit of prayer upon _____ (Acts 1:8; Romans 8:26). Send others to join us in praying for our pastor (1 Timothy 2:1-8). Amen.

22. Lord, keep my pastor in the fear of God. Let my pastor not fear people (Proverbs 19:23). Give _____ boldness to confront sin and church controllers. Honor my pastor's stand for you and come to his or her rescue. I claim Psalm 35 for my shepherd.

23. Lord, use _____ to renew our denomination (Proverbs 18:16). Use my pastor in an effective way to promote evangelism and holiness. Grant favor for fruitfulness. Keep my pastor from meetings for the sake

of meetings. Redeem the time so as to use my pastor's abilities in the most productive manner. Amen.

24. Lord give my pastor favor with his or her peers (Proverbs 11:4). Keep my pastor from comparing himself or herself with other pastors, churches or salary packages. Guard my pastor's heart from competition and unhealthy ambitions (2 Corinthians 10:18). Deliver _____ from the numbers trap, and give him or her a genuine concern for lost souls (Luke 19:10). Lord, you advance my pastor. Let my pastor not be caught up in any political quicksand; keep only Jacob's ladder, not a career ladder, before my pastor (Genesis 28:12). Amen.

25. Jesus, dominate _____ 's ministry to make people become like you and not like a denominational facsimile (Colossians 1:28). Amen.

> *Let my pastor not compromise truth, yet spread truth in love to address all social injustice and prejudice of any kind.*

26. Give my shepherd deep convictions and moral stands to reflect your holiness (Proverbs 4:20-27). Let my pastor not compromise truth, yet spread truth in love to address all social injustice and prejudice of any kind. Amen.

27. Let _____ trust in the Lord with all his or her heart. In all my pastor's ways may you be acknowledged and therefore, my pastor's paths made straight (James 1:5).

28. Bless my pastor with rich study time (Acts 6:4; 2 Timothy 2:15).

29. As _____ preaches, let him or her proclaim Jesus Christ (Colossians 1:28). Let my pastor's preaching be in the energy of the Holy Spirit. May we be presented to you, Father, holy and blameless as a result of my pastor's preaching. Amen.

30. Jesus, bless my pastor's preaching. Let my pastor preach Jesus

Christ. Let my pastor preach a revelation of Christ (1 Peter 1:7). And give my pastor ample opportunities to proclaim you (Colossians 4:3-4).

31. As your anointing teaches _____, teach us and admonish us in truth. Let your anointing be strong and powerful to convert the lost and convict the sinful (Luke 4:18; 1 John 2:27).

32. Lord by your Holy Spirit, anoint _____ to preach, and bring apostolic results (Acts 2:37). Let people be cut to the heart and accept Jesus Christ. Amen.

33. As my pastor speaks the word, let signs and wonders follow confirming it (Mark 16:20). Let the sick be healed; let the oppressed be set free. Anoint _____ with the truth (Matthew 16:17). With you, Lord, all things are possible.

34. Lord, as you have promised, grant my beloved shepherd lasting fruit (Malachi 3:11; John 15:16). Let my pastor's converts become disciples who in turn disciple. Bless my pastor with disciples who grow in the grace and knowledge of Jesus Christ.

35. God, I say that _____ will stand firm. Nothing will move my pastor (1 Corinthians 15:58). May my pastor always give himself or herself fully to your work because my pastor's labor is not in vain.

36. O Lord, take my pastor's hand so that he or she will not fear. Lead my pastor through difficult times. Let my pastor know that you are near and that you are my pastor's God. My pastor will not be dismayed. You will strengthen my pastor and help and uphold him or her with your righteous right hand (Isaiah 41:10).

37. O God, allow _____ to enter your rest (Hebrews 4; Matthew 11:28). Put your yoke on my pastor. When my pastor is heavily laden or burdened, may he or she find comfort and peace in you, refreshed and renewed by your power in every aspect of his or her life.

38. Father I thank you for _____ and for his or her call and gifts (Colossians 1:3-6). I praise you for sending such a shepherd for my soul! To you belong honor and glory. You are worthy, our Lord and God, to receive glory and honor and power, for you created all things, and by your will they were created and have their being (Revelation 4:11). Amen.

39. Lord make my pastor strong and filled with courage for every task (Joshua 1). Let my pastor lead us to inherit our city for you. Thank you for being with _____.

40. In Jesus' name, _____ shall fight the good fight of faith, fleeing from evil to God by pursuing righteousness, godliness, faith, love, endurance and gentleness (1 Timothy 6:12). I praise you, Lord, that you have taken hold of this special shepherd in the personal experience of eternal life. Amen.

THE FIRST PRAYED FOR PREACHERS

Jesus warned his followers, "If the world hates you, keep in mind that it hated me first," and, "If they persecuted me, they will persecute you also" (John 15:18, 20). He assured them they would have tribulation.

Therefore, it is little wonder that Jesus prayed on the eve of his departure for his pastors:

> I pray for them..., Holy Father, protect them by the power of your Name—the Name you gave me—so that they may be one as we are one.... My prayer is not that you take them out of the world but that you protect them from the evil one (John 17:9, 11, 15).

If Jesus saw the importance of this, we should too. If he prayed for the pastors, we should as well. In the New Testament, Jesus modeled prayer for pastors and the church followed his example. Praying for Paul or John was basically automatic.

Of course, the prayer life of the early church was so prevalent and important that they did not have to be told to pray. If they did not, they simply ceased to be. Read through the verses of Thessalonians and you will find a church that "prayed without ceasing," for in reality, they had little to distract them from personal and corporate prayer. They had no building program, no choir practice, no Bible studies (they had no Bible!), no policy or budget meetings, no annual convention. They just met in homes, orally adhered to the apostles' teaching, broke bread together, enjoyed fellowship and prayed. The leadership lived and ministered in an atmosphere of prayer.

> *The leadership lived and ministered in an atmosphere of prayer.*

Nothing ever started in the New Testament without prayer, including the pastors' ministries. They were bathed in it before being sent out. Pastors were prayed for from the very start. Pastor Paul got his start in ministry when Ananias laid hands on him and he was filled with the Holy Spirit. In Acts 14:23, Paul and Barnabas chose pastors for each church and then fasted and prayed and committed themselves to the Lord. Before Peter preached on the Day of Pentecost, the apostles met in the upper room and had a prayer meeting to invite the Holy Spirit. Peter's preaching was empowered by the saints in the upper room. This church knew how to pray for its preachers! Paul could say with confidence:

> Pray also for me, that whenever I open my mouth, words may be given me so that I will fearlessly make known the mystery of the gospel.... Pray that I may declare it fearlessly, as I should (Ephesians 6:19-20).

A prayed-for pastor is an anointed preacher!

The early church also met to pray whenever their pastors were in danger. In Acts 4, Peter and John had been threatened not to preach the name of Jesus. So the people prayed. "After they prayed, the place where they were meeting was shaken. They were all filled with the Holy Spirit and spoke the word of God boldly" (Acts 4:31).

These pastors did not face threats alone. When they were arrested and their lives endangered, the early church prayed to rescue them. In Acts 12:5 we read, "So Peter was kept in prison, but the church was earnestly praying to God for him." Then, as the story goes, an angel was sent to set Peter free. Someone has said, "The angel fetched Peter, but it was prayer that fetched the angel!"

Paul was quick to ask the church to pray for him, saying:

> I urge you, brothers, by our Lord Jesus Christ and by the love of the Spirit, to join me in my struggle by praying to God for me. Pray that I may be rescued from the unbelievers in Judea... (Romans 15:30).

Evidently the early church did pray for Paul, because he was rescued innumerable times. In fact, he once remarked:

> He has delivered us from such a deadly peril, and he will deliver us. On him we have set our hope that he will continue to deliver us, as you help us by your prayers (2 Corinthians 1:10).

Prayer from the church not only reinforced these pastors in the face of spiritual opposition, but at times it literally saved their lives.

The church also prayed for the people to receive their pastors' messages and for doors of opportunity to open. Again, Paul exhorted the church, "Devote yourselves to prayer, being watchful and thankful. And pray for us, too, that God may open a door for our message..." (Colossians 4:2-3). And God did open that door—again and again. When the church prayed, the pastors received direction, churches were planted and whole regions were evangelized.

A good example of this is in Acts 13 when Barnabas and Paul were set apart for their first missionary journey. The church was worshiping the Lord and fasting. They laid hands on their pastors and prayed for them and for the success of the mission. They became a part of their pastors' ministry by praying and fasting for open doors of opportunity.

Prayer was also offered to bring closure to a pastor's ministry. In Acts 20:17-38, Pastor Paul said goodbye to the church at Ephesus and he knelt down with all of them and prayed. Pastors were prayed for both coming and going!

One of the most touching scenes in the book of Acts demonstrated how highly committed the early church was to its pastors, and the power of prayer that resulted from their devotion. In Acts 14:19-20, Pastor Paul had preached in Lystra and had healed a lame man. The Jews became so angry that they came from Antioch, formed a mob and dragged Paul outside the city where they stoned him and left him for dead.

Imagine the grief the disciples

6. WHAT OTHER BIBLE PASSAGES OR BOOKS COULD YOU PRAY OVER YOUR SHEPHERD?

1.

2.

3.

7. DO YOU REALLY THINK IT IS POSSIBLE FOR YOUR PASTOR TO SEE THE KIND OF RESULTS DESCRIBED IN THE BOOK OF ACTS? EXPLAIN.

must have felt as they gathered around their beaten and bloodied pastor. They must have wept over him and cried out to God. In the midst of this display, Paul "got up and went back into the city."

Wow! There he lay under a pile of stones—dead. But the church gathered around him and prayed, and God raised him up.

The 28 chapters in the book of Acts tell story after story of the mighty acts of God in answer to prayer in the lives of pastors. Their preaching was powerful and fruitful; they healed the sick in Jesus' name; they met opposition with an increased faith in God. They were supernaturally empowered and they turned their world right-side up.

When they had money, they gave it away. Their joy was contagious, and whole cities were infected by it. They did the works of God, casting out demons and challenging the legalistic religious strongholds of the day. They met racism head-on and broke down its barriers. They ignited changed lives to spread the gospel fire even further. Riots could not stop them. Jails only made them pray and sing and win people to Christ. Snake bites only set the stage for healing. Stonings did not keep them from preaching and shipwrecks could not deter them.

These pastors and apostles stayed on the crest of the Holy Spirit's impetus. They were untouchable and unstoppable. "The Lord's hand was with them, and a great number of people believed and turned to the Lord" (Acts 11:21). Steeped in, empowered by and undergirded with prayer, these New Testament pastors were the "point men" for a kingdom advance that hasn't concluded yet.

CHAPTER SEVEN

BREAKTHROUGHS AND ———
Beachheads

Prayer hedges work. They work because they draw on the foundations of the new covenant, which was ratified and sealed on the cross. And they work because they honor those men and women whom God has sovereignly chosen to care for his bride.

Throughout much of this book, I have emphasized that facet of prayer hedges that is protective, shielding your pastor from all sorts of darts the enemy hurls at him. It is critical to your shepherd's survival that you understand this defensive strategy because the Bible guarantees that he will be persecuted and attacked. If he is not prayed for, he will be preyed on, and eventually chewed up.

I have also stressed that God wants to bless your pastor with rich study time, fresh visions and revelations, rewarding relationships, and especially lasting fruit. God has a special calling on your pastor's life, and wants nothing more than for him to be effective in ministry and to see his divine purpose through to completion.

Neither of these results can be achieved by inconsistent or crisis-oriented prayer. To be fully effective, prayer hedges must be organized and nurtured just like any other high-priority ministry in the church. They need leadership that is structured and goal-oriented, yet at the same time, compassionate, relational and sensitive to the direction of the Holy Spirit. They require mature, committed intercessors that understand the unique challenges inherent to the pastorate. In other words, they are not easy. They will not happen by chance or overnight.

However, the pastor who has a strong, healthy prayer hedge around him and his family has something more valuable than words on a page can communicate. All of the stories I have shared in this book represent real people and families—lives that were literally saved from destruction and courses that were changed through the prayers of people like you. Any pastor who has known both the joys of being prayed for and the pain of being shot at will tell you that prayer hedges can be hard work, but they are well worth the effort.

BREAKTHROUGHS AND BEACHHEADS

If I have accomplished my purpose in this book, then I have convinced you of both the need and the feasibility of a very "perspirational" kind of prayer force in behalf of your pastor. It is perspirational because it is not dependent on feelings or emotions, but rather a conscious commitment to a biblical model. I believe this kind of commitment should be the foundation on which you build your hedge so that it can weather the storms of apathy, doubt and resistance.

However, we all know that prayer has a very "inspirational" side also—those moments when you cry out to God in absolute despair over a problem that seems insurmountable, and then watch as he moves the mountain, or those times when you rejoice over a long-awaited answer to prayer. It is this inspirational side of prayer that seems to capture our hearts because we are naturally drawn to the passion and intensity.

As you build a prayer hedge around your pastoral family, you will begin to see exciting things happen in their lives and in the life of your church because of this spiritual principle: Fervent, ongoing prayer yields break-throughs and beachheads. It is these results that will become the celebrated rewards for those who pray.

> *Fervent, ongoing prayer yields breakthroughs and beachheads.*

Webster defines a breakthrough as "an act of breaking through a restriction or obstacle; a major achievement or discovery that permits further progress." At times, your prayers will be the force that pushes back a barrier, overcomes a hurdle, opens a closed door, or reveals a key insight.

In Acts 12, the early church received a breakthrough in answer to prayer when an angel was sent to free Peter from prison. Not only did the breakthrough answer a pressing need in Peter's life, it became a great source of encouragement to the church at a time when they needed something to be happy about! Breakthroughs inspire people to keep praying, especially when they become spiritual beachheads.

A spiritual beachhead is a specific kind of breakthrough, one that results in a significant foothold for truth and the gospel that has the potential to advance the kingdom of light. According to Webster, a beachhead is "an area on an enemy shoreline secured by troops in advance of an invading force." What a powerful concept!

The early church experienced a beachhead in Acts chapter 10 when

1. THINK OF A BREAKTHROUGH OR BEACHHEAD YOU HAVE SEEN AS A RESULT OF PRAYER. SHARE IT WITH YOUR GROUP.

2. WHAT KIND OF BREAKTHROUGH WOULD ENCOURAGE YOUR PASTOR RIGHT NOW? IS THERE AN OBSTACLE BLOCKING THE WAY TO AN IMPORTANT MINISTRY OBJECTIVE? BEGIN PRAYING RIGHT NOW FOR GOD TO INTERVENE.

Peter was invited by Cornelius to his home and Cornelius's entire household responded to the gospel message. Up until that point, it was believed that the gospel was only for the Jews. In fact, it was forbidden for Jews to even associate with Gentiles. But when God gave Peter the vision that led him to witness to the Gentile centurion and his family, the door to that entire people group was thrown opened. It happened, of course, in response to prayer.

In light of breakthroughs and beachheads, in this final chapter, I would like to share with you several of the most inspirational prayer hedge stories that I have witnessed. The important thing to note about these amazing testimonies though, is that none of them would have been likely to happen had there not *already* been a structured, intentional prayer covering over the pastors that experienced them. The dynamic breakthroughs that you are about to read were won by intercessors like yourself who were committed to praying for their leader long before crisis hit.

BRUCE OLSON AND THE MOTILONES

Poison arrows! That's what welcomed Bruce Olson when he entered the land of the Motilone Indians in Columbia, South America. Most missionaries would have turned and fled, but not Bruce. He persevered and eventually won the entire tribe to Jesus Christ. He also helped them build schools and clinics.

Unfortunately, not everyone appreciated Bruce's work. In 1989, he was captured by political terrorists and held for nine months. During that time, he witnessed the murder of six fellow hostages. Once, his captors placed him in front of a firing squad and shot blanks to frighten him.

While preparing to die, he prayed for his captors. He was finally released, unharmed. One of his first acts after gaining his freedom was to write an open letter to the thousands of intercessors around the world who had been praying for his safe return. These were his words:

> Your prayers had a profound effect. God heard and answered your petitions for me, for the Motilones, and even for my captors. The guerrillas may have believed in the beginning that it was they who controlled my fate, but in the end, more than sixty percent of my captors accepted the redeeming grace of Jesus Christ. They gladly attended the jungle schools I extemporaneously organized for them, where they learned to read and write and studied political and social sciences. I even taught them to cook—new ways with jungle cuisine! (Palm grubs and monkey entrails became their favorites.) As months passed, more and more guerrillas worshiped with me on Sundays. When I was close to death from intestinal hemorrhaging, guerrillas vied for the "honor" of donating their blood to save me. When I was near death on several occasions they wept for me and even risked their own lives by showing their sympathy for me.

Bruce was subjected to threats on his life that are too gruesome for most of us to comprehend. However, he seemed to experience one breakthrough after another in his efforts to evangelize the Motilone people. He had no doubt that the miraculous things he witnessed were a direct result of the many back home in the states that were praying in his behalf.

He was a modern day Paul—literally laying his life every day in the prayers of his intercessors for the sake of the gospel. Not only did Bruce Olson survive, he was blessed with much fruit for the kingdom in his adverse circumstances.

LIFE-SAVING INTERCESSION

One of my advisory board members and colleagues in the ministry is a pastor by the name of Jim Jackson. Currently serving the Chapelwood United Methodist Church in Houston, Texas, Jim has an amazing story to tell about a breakthrough that he experienced in a very unique way.

Several years ago, Jim was jogging in a neighborhood near his home when he heard a woman screaming from inside a house. It was a terrified scream, one that sent chills through his body and left no question in his mind that something was horribly wrong. Instinctively, he turned and ran up the sidewalk to see if he could help. Jim had no idea that he was heading into a violent ambush.

As he bounded up the stairs of the front porch, someone opened fire from inside the house, hitting the bewildered pastor six times in the chest area. Jim fell motionless to the ground.

When they arrived at the scene, paramedics didn't give Jim much of a chance for survival. But they transported him to the hospital where he was operated on for hours. He stayed unconscious, only barely alive, for several weeks.

Jim was good-natured and well-respected, so the event sent shock waves throughout the community. News of the tragedy spread almost instantly throughout Jim's 3,000 member church. A core of Jim's most faithful intercessors quickly organized a massive prayer hedge to plead for their pastor's life. In shifts, several of the pray-ers stayed at the hospital around the clock.

After weeks of intense prayer, touch-and-go reports from doctors, and fading hopes, Jim miraculously awoke. But what was even more amazing was the dream he relayed to his wife, Susan:

> It was very strange. I was hanging by a rope off the edge of steep cliff. I knew I couldn't hold on much longer, and that I was going to die. I felt desperate and hopeless. But then I looked up to the top of the cliff and I saw faces on the other end of the rope. They weren't nameless people, like you sometimes have in dreams. These were faces of specific people in our church, and I recognized them immediately—Kim, Cheryl, Donald, Patsy. I called out to them for help, but they just seemed to be looking at me.

When Susan heard this, she caught her breath and tears began to run down her face. "Those people you saw were the same people who have been here night and day praying for you, Jim. Those people wouldn't let you die—you were hanging on by nothing more than their prayers!"

> *"Those people wouldn't let you die—you were hanging on by nothing more than their prayers!"*

Today, Jim still carries one of the bullets in his body as a reminder of how the power of intercessory prayer was applied to his life. Neither he nor his prayer partners will ever question the importance or effectiveness of the hedge they have around him and his family.

A SPIRITUAL MANTLE

George Wickes had a love for people and a passion for the gospel that made him, in spite of his plain spoken, humble nature, somewhat of a legend in north Indiana. He was known by thousands and loved by just about every single one of them. He never forgot a name, and something about his pure, joyful spirit transcended every barrier, drawing people of all ages and colors to him. Throughout the decades that he worked as a lay witness missionary, he led hundreds, probably thousands of people to the Lord, and inspired several hundred more into full time ministry.

Although there was nothing "hip" about George, he had a profound affect on young people. The bands of teens that traveled along with him on lay witness mission trips to share their own testimonies were the most sold-out young people you can imagine, and they loved George. He had a special anointing to reach them, inspire them, and motivate them to Christlikeness.

One of George's converts was a young man I mentioned earlier named Gregg Parris, who traveled with George on a mission trip at the age of 18. He, like many, was called into ministry and today, pastors one of Muncie, Indiana's largest churches. Gregg too, has a passion for influencing the lost for Christ, and has always had a special desire to reach the youth of his area and see them changed by the gospel.

Gregg's youth program at Union Chapel had, like most youth groups, rocked along for several years without seeing a net gain. It was a good program—kids came and went, and some good things happened, but they just weren't having the impact Gregg had envisioned in the community. They were doing an adequate job of ministering to the youth of the church families, but they weren't reaching kids outside the church. They weren't seeing teens converted. Gregg wanted to see a breakthrough, and it came about through a youth program called "One-Eighty" and a hospital prayer.

Like so many people in the area, Gregg held a special place for George in his life as a spiritual father and mentor. So when George became ill a couple of years ago and was hospitalized, Gregg went to see him. As he sat beside the bed where his friend lay dying, he said, "George, I want what you've got. Pray for me, so that I can receive your mantle for soul-winning. You're not going to need it anymore." And with that, Gregg stretched out across George's feeble body as George laid hands on him and prayed.

> "I want what you've got. Pray for me, so that I can receive your mantle for soul-winning. You're not going to need it anymore."

There were no bells or whistles. No visions or strange sensations. Gregg left the hospital that day feeling much the same as when he had arrived, and several days later, George Wickes went on to be with Jesus.

Within weeks, however, Gregg noticed something remarkable. The attendance at their Sunday night youth meetings suddenly began to rise—sharply. First it doubled, then, it quadrupled. At their kick-off of the "One-Eighty" youth program they had been planning to implement, just weeks after George died, 500 teenagers packed out the youth building, and 48 received Christ! Within six months, they had gone from an average of 80-100 in youth group, to seeing 300-400 teenagers every Sunday night.

And not only were the numbers increasing, so was the fruit. Every week came reports of more teens that were being saved, many from unchurched families. They began bussing in young people from all parts of the community, especially low-income neighborhoods. Today, Union Chapel's "One-Eighty" continues to average 500-600 teens every Sunday night, has recorded hundreds of professions of faith in the past year and a half, and has become recognized as one of the most effective, dynamic youth ministries in the country.

Now I suppose it's difficult to say exactly what made the youth program suddenly take off at Union Chapel. Maybe it was effective marketing; perhaps it was the new program. Or maybe it was just coincidence. But if you ask Gregg Parris why all those teenagers suddenly took over an entire wing of his building, he will take you back to George Wickes and the prayer he received in the St. Elizabeth Hospital.

I believe, as does Gregg, that he received a mantle that day—a divine anointing to attract and impact youth and set them on fire for Jesus. George's prayer established a beachhead for Gregg in his community, setting the stage for spiritual victory in the lives of hundreds of young people who had never even been to church.

> *A simple prayer, a strategic foothold and a sudden move of the Holy Spirit. Who's laying hands on your pastor?*

A simple prayer, a strategic foothold and a sudden move of the Holy Spirit. Who's laying hands on your pastor?

"GRACIAS, ADIOS!"

Before accepting his current position as president of Southeastern College in Lakeland, Florida, Mark Rutland traveled extensively throughout the United States and abroad as a guest preacher and evangelist. His razor-sharp intellect and quick sense of humor made him a highly sought after speaker in all kinds of churches, rallies and seminars. He especially loved Mexico.

One of Mark's goals was to be the most prayed for evangelist alive. Everywhere he went, he recruited people to pray for him and his family. He called his hedge the "Elijah Force," and they were scattered among several nations. He communicated with them diligently, and their prayers surrounded him every time he stood up to speak.

Despite Mark's frequent trips to Mexico, a handful of words was about all he knew how to say in Spanish—just enough to string together two or three sentences of greeting. That never concerned him, though. He did fine preaching through interpreters, although the translation process always slowed him down a bit and all but nullified his sense of humor. He could no doubt have learned the language, but in the small burros where he traveled, a textbook version of Spanish probably would not have done him much good anyway. To become fluent enough to preach effectively would have required years of study and practice.

Then one afternoon, Mark experienced an amazing breakthrough that profoundly changed his ministry. In a remote mountain village southwest of Tampico, the Holy Spirit did something very unusual.

Mark and several other Americans were supposed to be involved in a church service, but the interpreter who was coming over from the city never arrived because the bus he was riding broke down. None of the Americans spoke enough Spanish to fill in, and no one in the village spoke a word of English. Frustrated, they had no options. In what Mark describes as a "painful, stumbling conference with several Mexicans," they decided the pastor of the church should preach, and that Mark would simply give a greeting—all he could do with no one to translate.

But when Mark stood to wave a regretful "adios," out of his own mouth poured native Spanish, and for 35 minutes, he preached with complete ease and confidence. In that miraculous moment, he received instant access to the entire Spanish language.

It is hard to say who was more delighted by the surprise, Mark or his audience. And while he doesn't exactly know how to explain what he experienced that day, he says this:

> Whatever happened, it was a miracle of communication. In that moment of need, the Holy Spirit gifted

3. IS IT UNREALISTIC OR OLD-
FASHIONED TO THINK THAT A
GROUP OF MEN AND WOMEN
COULD SUPPORT A SPIRITUAL
LEADER LIKE THE GIBBORIUM
SUPPORTED DAVID, EVEN TO THE
POINT OF DEATH?

4. WILL YOU COMMIT TODAY TO
BE AN "AMASAI" IN YOUR
SHEPHERD'S LIFE?

me with Spanish that I speak today. As it began to dawn on all in the church what was happening, the Mexicans and the Americans began to weep in the presence of the Lord. What a night! Seeing the power of God, many were saved and baptized in the Holy Spirit in that place (59-60).

To this day, Mark can speak and understand fluent Spanish, but he can not read nor write a word of it. He could not conjugate a verb to save his life. God simply blessed him with a linguistic gift that established a beachhead in his ministry. Many lives were impacted with the gospel message because of the miracle, not just that day, but for years afterward as Mark continued to be faithful to his calling in Mexico.

Ask any of these men—Bruce, Jim, Gregg, Mark—"How important is prayer to your ministry?" They will tell you that it is the single most important factor to their survival and success. It is that mysterious force that keeps them squarely in the will and provision of the Father. It is a protective shield, and a conduit of breakthroughs, beachheads and blessings.

WE ARE YOURS!

David was perhaps the most transparent leader portrayed in the Bible. A shepherd, a warrior, a musician and a king, David recorded some of his most intimate thoughts in the book of Psalms. He honestly declared both the anguish that often gripped his soul, and the passion with which he continually worshiped God. He wrote:

> O Lord, how many are my foes! How many rise up against me! ...My thoughts trouble me and I am distraught at the voice of the enemy, at the stares of the wicked; for they bring down suffering upon me.... Fear and trembling have beset me; horror has overwhelmed me (Psalm 3:1; 55:2-5).

> I will extol the Lord at all times; his praise will always be on my lips. My soul will boast in the Lord; let the afflicted hear and rejoice.... I will praise you as long as I live, and in your name I will lift up my hands (Psalm 34:1-2, 63:4).

So how was David able to maintain such a heart of praise in the face of all the dangers and hardships that plagued his life? David had an incredible prayer hedge.

About 600 strong, David's "Gibborium," the Hebrew word for "mighty men," supported David during his entire rule as king. They went where he went, slept where he slept, and protected and cared for him like their own flesh. They were a source of blessing for David throughout his life. Old and battle-scarred, they surrounded him even as he died, pledging their support to his son, Solomon, their new king (1 Chronicles 29:24).

Listen to the loyalty of Amasai, one of David's mighty men:
    We are yours, O David!
    We are with you, O son of Jesse!
    Success, success to you,
    and success to those who help you,
    for your God will help you" (1 Chronicles 12:18).

Is anyone saying that to your pastor? Can you build a hedge of mighty men and women who will lift up your pastor's hands and be the difference between success and failure? Honor God by praying for your shepherd and great will be your reward.

FIFTY WAYS TO PROMOTE ___
Prayer for Pastors

1. Each Sunday name a different church and pastor in the bulletin. Ask the congregation pray for them sometime during the week.

2. Churches in a District or Association can exchange names and prayer requests of pastors and pray for them. Give the prayer exercise a time limit and share answered prayer.

3. Organize a men's group to pray with and for the pastor.

4. If your church has a prayer room, put a picture of the pastor in it to remind people to pray.

5. Ask your church administrative board to budget an annual prayer retreat for the pastor.

6. Help your pastor find a weekly prayer retreat place.

7. Keep the names of your denominational leaders on the prayer list,

perhaps in your bulletin.

8. Solicit the women's group to pray for the pastor and his family. Encourage them to do a book study on *Preyed On or Prayed For*.

9. Have the pastor fill out a pastor's prayer request form and distribute it each week to groups that are praying.

10. Encourage your pastor to pray with other pastors.

11. Start Sunday school classes with prayer time for the pastor.

12. Encourage weekly cell groups to spend time praying for the pastor and his upcoming message. Provide them with sermon texts or scriptures so they can pray specifically.

13. Provide the youth groups with a prayer guide for the pastor. Youth groups are powerful in prayer.

14. Have a lay leader in the church pray for the pastor during worship each Sunday.

15. Have different classes or small groups study *Preyed On or Prayed For*.

16. Have church members write out prayers based on scriptures and then mail them to their pastor. These prayer letters encourage pastors.

17. Open the sanctuary early on Sunday for people to come and pray for the pastor.

18. Make available a list of all the pastors and churches in your city and ask your congregation to pray for them.

19. Conduct a twenty-four hour prayer vigil twice a year. Sign up people to come on Saturday for one hour time slots to intercede for the shepherd.

20. Lead groups in *Acts 29 Fifty Days to Invite the Holy Spirit*.

21. Ask the youth group to baby-sit the pastor's kids free so the pastor and his wife can be alone with God.

22. If your church has a church staff, promote prayer for each staff member. Encourage the staff to pray for each other and to have corporate prayer time.

23. Teach the members of your church to pray over the pastor and his family when they have their evening meal.

24. Encourage the choir or musicians sitting behind the pastor to pray while he preaches. Teach them to pray short prayers like, "Help him, Lord," and, "Holy Spirit quicken him as he gives the invitation."

25. Stress the importance of "pew-praying" for the pastor. As people come in, they can say a short prayer for him, and during the service, they can pray especially during the invitation.

26. Ask the ushers to pray as they present the offering. Prayer modeling facilitates congregational praying for leaders.

27. Teach the small children in Sunday school how to pray for the pastor.

28. Remind your administrative board to pray for the minister. The board may assign this prayer task each meeting to a different leader so he can prepare a prayer for the pastor.

29. Give out table cards that remind people to pray for the pastor during their prayer time. These are available from Prayer Point Press or you can design your own.

30. Publish the pastor's vision so members can pray for it to be fulfilled.

31. Remind people to pray for the pastor in all written communications, like newsletters or bulletins.

32. Once a year, bring your pastor and his family to the altar to lay hands on them and renew the church's commitment to pray for them.

33. Print Bible book markers with the church's denominational leadership listed along with local church staff so people can pray for them

by name.

34. Periodically pass out prayer guides to help people pray for the pastor.

35. Print some bumper stickers to read, "Have you prayed for your pastor today?" This lifts community awareness to pray for all pastors.

36. Remind your pastor to inform the church when he has a funeral so they can pray at the exact hour he stands up to comfort the family.

37. Encourage prayer at district or area pastor's meetings. This can be a time for pastors to share those things that have hurt them and receive prayer from their peers.

38. Give the retired pastors in your community a list of current pastors and their needs to pray over.

39. Organize a city wide day of prayer for pastors.

40. List the pastors prayer concerns on voice mail, so people can call and find out how to pray.

41. Call the Oral Roberts Prayer Tower (918/495-6807) and ask them to pray for your pastor to be a great soul winner and discipler.

42. Inform your pastor about the Renewal Ministries email prayer line for pastors at <http://www.renewalministries.com>.

43. Circulate a list of local prison or hospital chaplains so they can be prayed for. Pastors who have no church desperately need prayer.

44. Call the Upper Room in Nashville, Tennessee, (615/340-7215) and give them a brief prayer list for your pastor to be lifted up.

45. Use objects and sites to remind people in the church to pray at random. For example, teach your fellow members that every time they pass a church, they could say a short prayer for their own shepherd. Or, if your pastor likes golf, they could put a golf ball in their car, and pray for him every time they touch the ball or drive by a golf course.

46. Use church bulletin boards to remind people to pray for the staff or pastor. The artist in the church could create beautiful ways to spark prayer for the shepherd.

47. On the National Day of Prayer in May, gather at pulpits in your area to pray for pastors and a strong message of revival and holiness in the land.

48. Share prayer materials that teach the importance of prayer.

49. Start an "Aaron and Hur Society" to lift up the pastor's hands and promote camaraderie to pray for the shepherd.

50. Simply and spontaneously thank God for your pastor often because he is a special gift from God to you and your church.

APPENDIX B

HEDGING IN THE PASTOR ——
Prayer Guide

HEDGING IN THE PASTOR
Ephesians 6:10-18

"Be strong in the Lord and the strength of his might." Ephesians 6:10

MEDITATE   on the greatness of God in behalf of your pastor. Romans 8:28, 31, 37, 1 Peter 3:12

EXPOSE   the wiles of the devil. Ephesians 6:11-12

CLAIM   scriptural promises for your pastor's overall protection. Isaiah 54:14-17, Psalm 34:7, Psalm 91, Luke 10:19, 2 Corinthians 10:3-4

PETITION   the Father to grant _____ a discerning spirit. 2 Corinthians 11:14, 1 John 4:1

THE PASTOR'S PRIVATE LIFE
"Stand, therefore, girded in truth." Ephesians 6:14

REQUEST   that your shepherd's glory be solely in the cross. Galatians 6:14

PRAY   for continued rest and renewal. Isaiah 40:27-31, Hebrews 4:1-13
              for holiness. 1 Peter 1:16

SEEK   for _____ a clear vision of the merits of Christ. Philippians 3:7-10
              for godly contentment. 1 Timothy 6:6
              for the love of God to be shed abroad in his/her heart. Romans 5:5

THE PASTOR'S PERSONAL LIFE
"Stand, ...having put on the breastplate of righteousness." Ephesians 6:14

INTERCEDE   for your pastor's spouse and children. Psalm 91:9-12, Psalm 37:25

CANCEL   in Jesus' name all assignments against them. Matthew 16:19

REMOVE   by faith all obstacles to their total health and prosperity. Mark 11:23, Philippians 4:19

THE PASTOR'S PRAISE LIFE
"Stand, ...having shod your feet with the equipment of the gospel of peace."
Ephesians 6:15

ASK   the Father to give your shepherd strong worship. Matthew 4:10

BIND   the spirits of fear, gloom, and negativity. John 14:1, Isaiah 61:3, 2 Timothy 1:6-7

LISTEN   for any other direction to pray. Ecclesiastes 5:1-2

THE PASTOR'S PRAYER LIFE
"Stand, ...above all taking the shield of faith, with which you can quench all the flaming darts of the evil one." Ephesians 6:16

QUENCH   darts of doubt through the power of the Holy Spirit. Mark 6:5-6

REBUKE   all distractions from _____'s devotional time. Mark 5:36
LOOSEN   the forces of heaven to aid your pastor in prayer.
                         Mark 1:35 (private prayer)
                         Acts 1:14 (corporate prayer)

THE PASTOR'S PROFESSIONAL LIFE
"Stand, ...taking the helmet of salvation." Ephesians 6:17
SHIELD   my pastor from the fear of men. Isaiah 11:1-3, Proverbs 19:23
BESTOW   on _____ favor in the cities and nations. Proverbs 18:16
                on him/her support from local churches. Proverbs 11:4
ENTREAT   Jesus to give your leader an uncompromising truth. Proverbs 4:20-27
                Jesus to give him/her wisdom in leadership. James 1:5

THE PASTOR'S PREACHING LIFE
"Stand, ...with the sword of the spirit, which is the word of God." Ephesians 6:17
BLESS   _____ with rich study time. Acts 6:4, 2 Timothy 2:15
GRANT   my pastor a bold proclamation of Jesus. Colossians 1:28
                my pastor opportunities to impact whole areas for Christ.
                Colossians 4:3-4
ANOINT   my shepherd to minister the grace of God. Luke 4:18, 1 John 2:27
                him/her for apostolic results. Acts 2:37
                _____ for signs and wonders. Mark 16:20
                my pastor to reveal truth. Matthew 16:17

THE PASTOR'S PERSEVERING LIFE
"Stand, ...pray at all times in the spirit, with all prayer and supplication.
To that end keep alert with all perseverance...." Ephesians 6:18
HONOR   my pastor with lasting fruit in the nations. Malachi 3:11, John 15:16
CONFESS   steadfastness over him/her. 1 Corinthians 15:58
                bold vision for your spiritual leader. Isaiah 41:10
                rest and times of refreshing for him/her. Hebrews 4, Matthew 11:28
GIVE   thanks for his/her call and gifts. Colossians 1:3-5
SECURE   _____ in courage. Joshua 1

"Fight the good fight of faith."
1 Timothy 6:12
EXPECT   all that you have prayed.
STAND   behind the pastor's family, girding them consistently in prayer.
YIELD   to the Spirit for other areas of prayer and intercession.

AMEN

HEDGING IN THE PASTOR
Ephesians 6:10-18

"Be strong in the Lord and in his mighty power." Ephesians 6:10

MEDITATE on the greatness of God on behalf of your pastor (Romans 8:28-37, 1 Peter 3:12). To meditate is to ponder in prayer some great theme about God—his holiness, greatness, grace, etc. Let this thought yield a rich revelation to apply to your pastor. For example:

> I thank you Father that your eyes are on my shepherd and your ears are attentive to my pastor's prayers and your face is against those who plot evil against _____ (1 Peter 3:12). For I know that in all things you work for the good of my pastor who loves you (Romans 8:28). Will you not graciously give him or her this city for Christ? And who can accuse this pastor who is daily interceded for by Christ Jesus? (Romans 8:32-34). Therefore, in all things my pastor is more than a conqueror (Romans 8:37). Thank God.

EXPOSE the wiles of the devil. (Ephesians 6:11-12).

CLAIM scriptural promises for their overall protection (Isaiah 54:14-17, Psalm 34:7, Psalm 91, Luke 10:19, and 2 Corinthians 10:3-5). Here is an example:

> Father, I thank you that no weapons formed against my shepherd will prosper. Every tongue raised against my leader will be cast down. Rumors and gossip will be turned aside. For _____ will be still before the Lord and will wait on you. My pastor will dwell in the shelter of the Most High God and will be delivered from terror, darts of doubt (Psalm 9:15), and diseases (Psalm 91:6). Set your

angels about him or her (Psalm 91:11) and no power of the enemy shall harm _____ (Luke 10:19). Thank God forevermore!

PETITION the Father to grant your pastor a discerning spirit (2 Corinthians 11:14, 1 John 4:1). Petition God:

Lord let my pastor have a discerning mind to set priorities. Let _____ discern what is most important and guard him or her from the tyranny of the urgent.

THE PASTOR'S PRIVATE LIFE
"Stand firm then, with the belt of truth buckled around your waist...."
Ephesians 6:14

As listed below, there are six areas to cover when praying for your pastor's private life. You may want to focus on one or two at a time. The Holy Spirit will help you pray correctly and on target (Romans 8:26). Nevertheless, circle your leader with truth. Simply pray or say out loud these truths as applied to one of these areas.

REQUEST that your pastor's glory be solely in the cross (Galatians 6:14) and that your pastor's private life be kept intact as he or she stays close to the cross. The cross guards a shepherd from pride, self-promotion, presumption and the need for reward and attention. The enemy is totally defenseless against the cross of Christ.

PRAY for your pastor's continued renewal (Isaiah 40:27-31). Pray

to the Father:

> **Renew my pastor in the Holy Spirit. Let him or her hope in you and soar on wings like eagles. Quicken his or her body with the Holy Spirit (Romans 8:11). Renew _____ 's vision and confidence (1 John 5:13-14). Revive his or her boldness to stand in strong personal conviction (Acts 5:42). Amen.**

PRAY for holiness (1 Peter 1:16).

> **Jesus, keep my pastor holy in every way. Keep him or her from seducing spirits, especially when tired and hard-pressed. Give my pastor comrades to share with in personal holiness (James 4:7). As _____ draws near to you, draw near to him or her (James 4:8). Cancel the power of sin to have no effect (Ephesians 1:22). Amen.**

SEEK for your pastor a clear vision of the merits of Christ (Philippians 3:7-11).

> I pray that the eyes of my pastor may be enlightened to know the hope to which we are called and know the riches of his or her glorious inheritance in the saints. Let my pastor know the incomparable great power that is in us who believe (Ephesians 1:18-19). Let _____ see the full revelation of Jesus Christ (Galatians 1:12) and place in my pastor a desire to know Christ and the power of his resurrection (Philippians 3:10). Amen.

SEEK God for godly contentment (1 Timothy 6:6).

> Lord deliver Pastor _____ from the tyranny of the unfinished. Grant him or her a sense of fulfillment and the personal joy of Jesus (1 Timothy 6:6, John 15:11). Amen.

SEEK for the love of God to be poured out into our hearts (Romans 5:5).

THE PASTOR'S PERSONAL LIFE
"Stand with the breastplate of righteousness in place...." Ephesians 6:14

As Christians we are saved by grace and we are made righteous through Jesus Christ (2 Corinthians 5:21). Further, we are to reign in this life through this gift of righteousness (Romans 5:17). We are blessed and guarded by our total right standing before God. Every prayer we pray is answered because of Jesus Christ. "The prayer of a righteous man is powerful and effective" (James 5:16). Therefore, this gift of righteousness protects and blesses our vitality as Christians.

INTERCEDE for your pastor's spouse, children and families (Psalm 91:9-12, 37:25).

> Lord, I lift up the hands of _____ (list your pastor's family members) as well as my pastor. Place them in the shelter of the Most High to rest in the shadow of the Almighty. I will say of the Lord, you are their refuge and fortress. You will preserve their family time. You will cover their home. Your faithfulness will meet their financial needs in Christ Jesus (Philippians 4:19). You will command your angels to guard them as they travel and win the lost. You have said, "I will be with them in trouble, I will deliver them and honor them and with a long life I will satisfy them and show them my salvation" (Psalm 91). Amen.

CANCEL in Jesus' name all assignments against your pastor (Matthew 16:9).

> Father, in Jesus' name and by his authority, I cancel any plot of the enemy to undo my shepherd's home. I stand against curses and schemes set against their

homes (Matthew 10:1). Guard them from friendly fire, accusations and gossip (Revelation 12:10-12). I resist the devil on their behalf, and he will flee (1 Peter 5:9, James 4:7). Amen.

REMOVE by faith all obstacles to your pastor's total health and prosperity (Mark 11:23, Philippians 4:19).

In Jesus' name I speak to church related hurts, abuse and ungrateful forces to move. I speak to mountains of criticism and inordinate expectations to be cast into the sea. I speak to stress, excessive phone counseling and fatigue to be cast into the sea. I believe every need, vision and dream will be completed (Mark 11:25, Philippians 4:19). Amen.

Forgive those who hurt our pastor and parsonage family and speak against them. May they walk in forgiveness (Ephesians 4:32, 5:1). Guard them from futile thinking (Ephesians 4:17) and vain imaginations. Let every thought be taken captive to obey Christ (2 Corinthians 10:3-5).

THE PASTOR'S PRAISE LIFE
"Stand... with your feet fitted with the readiness that comes from the gospel of peace." Ephesians 6:15

ASK the Father to give your pastor strong worship (Matthew 4:10).

> Lord Jesus, I know that in the course of pastoring, my pastor is thrilled over conversions and changed lives, yet I also realize that he or she hears bad news and sad stories. Therefore, keep my pastor ever before your face in worship. Let him or her see you and enjoy your presence ever more (Psalm 112:7). Let goodness and mercy follow my pastor all the days of his or her life (Psalm 23:6). Let this pastor's cup overflow (Psalm 23:50). Amen.

BIND the spirit of fear (John 14:1).

BIND the spirit of despair (Isaiah 61:3).

BIND the spirit of negativity (2 Timothy 1:7).

> Jesus, you said, "Do not let your hearts be troubled. Trust in God; trust also in me.... Peace I leave with you; my peace I give you" (John 14:1, 27). Apply these promises to my pastor. Let my pastor know the plans you have for him or her: plans to prosper, plans to give hope and a future (Jeremiah 29:11). Amen.

LISTEN for any other direction to pray (Ecclesiastes 5:1-2).

> Keep my pastor in the midst of good and exciting worship. Keep him or her from the traditions of humankind and religion which hold the form of godliness, but deny its power (2 Timothy 3:5). Give _____ a vision of heaven (Isaiah 6, Revelation 4). Amen.

THE PASTOR'S PRAYER LIFE

"Take up the shield of faith, with which you can extinguish all the flaming arrows of the evil one." Ephesians 6:16

The Roman shield was big. It covered the whole body. Roman soldiers used this shield to form a wall to deflect enemy arrows that were sometimes lit. Satan knows the flammable areas in our lives and he aims for them. He shoots us where it hurts. The shield represents faith. Faith covers all. My faith with your faith puts a wall around the pastor to protect and bless. Pray with this in mind.

QUENCH in the Holy Spirit darts of doubt (Mark 6:5-6).

REBUKE distractions from your pastor's devotional life (Mark 5:36).

LOOSEN the forces of heaven to aid in prayer (Mark 1:35, Acts 1:14).

> Lord, I stand against the enemies of my pastor's prayer life—busy-ness (Acts 6:4), compulsions, compromise (Acts 5), unnecessary phone calls, chronic counselees, fatigue, sleepiness (Matthew 26:41), appetites, television, late meetings, over-commitments and doubt. Let nothing hinder _____'s time with you. Let him or her rise up to seek you (Mark 1:35), pray with other pastors (Acts 1:14) and pray continually (1 Thessalonians 5: 17). Give my pastor the time, the desire and the place to pray (Acts 16:16). Amen.
>
> Send the spirit of prayer upon our pastor (Acts 1:8, Romans 8:26). Amen.
>
> Send others to join us in praying for our leader (1 Timothy 2:1-8). Amen.

THE PASTOR'S PROFESSIONAL LIFE
"Take the helmet of salvation...." Ephesians 6:17

SHIELD my pastor from the fear of men (Isaiah 11:2-3, Proverbs 19:23).

Proverbs says the fear of man is a snare and the fear of the Lord leads to life (Proverbs 29:25).

> Lord, keep my pastor in the fear of God. Let him or her not fear mere human beings. Give _____ boldness to confront sin and church controllers. Honor my pastor's stand for you. Come to his or her rescue. Claim Psalm 35 for your pastor.

BESTOW on my pastor favor in the denomination (Proverbs 18: 16).

BESTOW upon _____ support from his or her peers (Proverbs 11:4).

> Lord, keep my pastor from feeling competitive with other pastors, churches or salary packages. Guard his or her heart from unhealthy ambitions (2 Corinthians 10:18). Deliver my pastor from the numbers trap and give him or her a genuine concern for lost souls (Luke 19:10). Lord, advance my pastor. Let _____ not be caught up in any political quicksand, but keep only Jacob's ladder ever before my shepherd (Genesis 28:12). Amen.

> Lord Jesus, dominate my pastor's ministry so he or she will help people become like you instead of a denominational facsimile (Colossians 1:28). Amen.

ENTREAT Jesus to give your pastor an uncompromising truth (Proverbs 4:20-27).

ENTREAT wisdom in leadership (James 1:5).

THE PASTOR'S PREACHING LIFE
"Take the sword of the Spirit, which is the word of God."
Ephesians 6:17

BLESS my pastor with rich study time (Acts 6:4, 2 Timothy 2:15).

> **Lord, let my pastor come before you as one approved, a workman who does not need to be ashamed, who correctly handles the word of truth (2 Timothy 2:15). Amen.**

GRANT my pastor a bold proclamation of Jesus (Colossians 1:28).

GRANT my pastor many opportunities to proclaim the mystery of Christ (Colossians 4:3-4).

> **Jesus, bless my pastor's preaching. Let him or her preach Jesus Christ (Colossians 1:28). Let my pastor preach a revelation of Christ (1 Peter 1:7). And give this pastor ample opportunities to proclaim the good news (Colossians 4:3-4). Amen.**

ANOINT my pastor to preach and teach (Luke 4:18, 1 John 2:27).

ANOINT my pastor's preaching for apostolic results (Acts 2:37).

> **Lord, by your Holy Spirit anoint _____ to preach. Let people be cut to the heart to repent and accept Jesus Christ (Acts 2:37). Amen.**

ANOINT my pastor for signs and wonders (Mark 16:20).

ANOINT my pastor to reveal truth (Matthew 16:17).

THE PASTOR'S PERSEVERING LIFE

"Pray in the Spirit on all occasions with all kinds of prayers and requests. With this in mind, be alert and always keep on praying for all the saints." Ephesians 6:18

HONOR my pastor with lasting fruit (Malachi 3:11, John 15:16).

CONFESS steadfastness over your pastor (1 Corinthians 15:58).

CONFESS bold vision (Isaiah 41:10).

CONFESS rest (Hebrews 4, Matthew 11:28).

GIVE thanks for your pastor's call and gifts (Colossians 1:3-5).

> **Father, I thank you for my pastor. I praise you for sending such a shepherd for my soul. To you belong honor and glory. You are worthy, our Lord and God, to receive glory and honor and power, for you created all things, and by your will they were created and have their being (Revelation 4:11). Amen.**

SECURE your pastor in courage (Joshua 1).

FIGHT the good fight of faith (1 Timothy 6:12).

EXPECT all that you have prayed.

STAND behind your pastor, encircling him or her in prayer.

YIELD to the Spirit for other areas of prayer and intercession.

WORKS CITED

George Barna. Barna Research Group. 20 Sept. 2000. Online posting. Press release 21 Dec. 1999. < http://www.barna.org >

George Barna. Today's Pastors. Ventura, CA: Regal Books, 1993.

Alfred H. Ells. *Counselor's Corner*. A publication of ClergyCare, Mesa, Arizona. 3.9 (2000).

General Board of Global Ministries. Official records from the United Methodist Church research office. New York: 2000.

Dudley Hall. *Out of the Comfort Zone*. Pineville, NC: Morning Star, 1991.

Cindy Jacobs. Possessing the Gates of the Enemy. Grand Rapids: Baker Book House, 1993.

Reginald Klimionok. *How to Put on God's Armour*. Franklin Springs, GA: Advocate Press, 1988.

Ralph W. Neighbour, Jr. *Where Do We Go From Here?* Houston: Touch Publications, 1990.

Newsweek. "Priests and Abuse." 16 Aug. 1993.

Mark Rutland. *Launch out into the Deep*. 3rd ed. Lakeland, FL: T.F.P., a division of Global Servants, 1999.

Terry Teykl. *Keys to the Kingdom: Prayers for my Pastor*. Muncie, IN: Prayer Point Press, 1997.

C. Peter Wagner. *Prayer Shield*. Ventura, CA: Regal Books, 1992.

C. Peter Wagner. *Warfare Prayer*. Ventura, CA: Regal Books, 1982.